A Perfect Friend

A Perfect Friend

The Life of Cumbrian Plant Hunter

WILLIAM PURDOM

O. V. Presant

HAYLOFT

First published by Hayloft Publishing Ltd., 2019

A CIP catalogue record for this book is available from the British Library

ISBN 978-1-910237-47-2

Designed, printed and bound in the EU

Hayloft policy is to use papers that are natural, renewable and recyclable products and made from wood grown in sustainable forests. The logging and manufacturing processes are expected to conform to the environmental regulations of the country of origin.

This book is printed with the offset of carbon emissions and support for Forest Protection, Pará, Brazil.

Climate neutral
Print product
ClimatePartner.com/12667-1803-1003

Hayloft Publishing Ltd,
a company registered in England number 4802586
2 Staveley Mill Yard, Staveley, Kendal, LA8 9LR (registered office)
L'Ancien Presbytère, 21460 Corsaint, France (editorial office)

Email: books@hayloft.eu
Tel: 07971 352473
www.hayloft.eu

Frontispiece: Purdom family in 1897, photograph courtesy of Alan Purdom.

For Don
and
The Lakeland Horticultural Society

without whom this book could not have been written

and

The Purdom Forest Park
China

where William Purdom is commemorated to this day

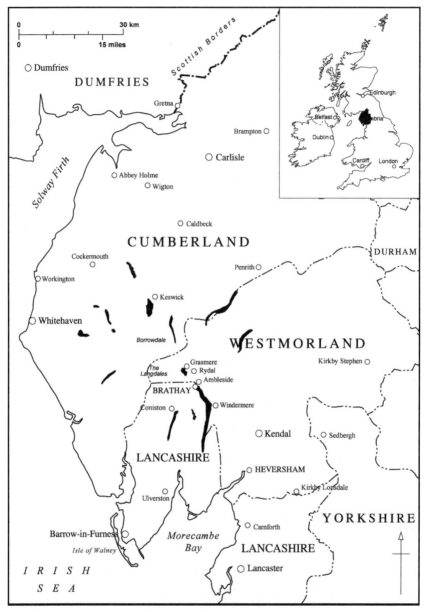

Cumbria was created in 1974 from the counties of Cumberland, Westmorland and that part of Lancashire north of Morecambe Bay

Contents

'If ever a traveller was luckier than I in his friend,
I've never yet heard it, and don't believe it.'

Reginald Farrer, *On the Eaves of the World*

'One of the most beautiful qualities of true friendship
is to understand and to be understood.'

Lucius Annaeus Seneca

How it all Began

Run entirely by volunteers the gardens of the Lakeland Horticultural Society in Windermere, offer much to workers and visitors alike; companionship certainly, but also the opportunity to learn and share knowledge through talks, courses or just being there.

An old seat in the sunshine may seem a strange place to inspire a biography. It carried a then almost illegible plaque:

For Three Native Lakeland Gardeners,
William Purdom and sons William and Harry.

After 40 years the original seat has worn away but its replacement carries the same plaque and remains in its original position overlooking Windermere towards Brathay.

Why was there a Purdom bed nearby? Who had donated the seat? Above all who were the Purdoms?

The Purdom Family Tree

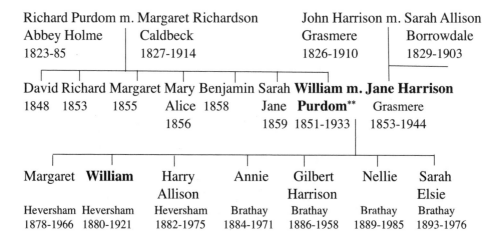

Richard Purdom m. Margaret Richardson   John Harrison m. Sarah Allison
Abbey Holme | Caldbeck   Grasmere | Borrowdale
1823-85 | 1827-1914   1826-1910 | 1829-1903

David Richard Margaret Mary Benjamin Sarah **William m. Jane Harrison**
1848   1853   1855   Alice 1858   Jane **Purdom**** Grasmere
                        1856   1859 1851-1933 | 1853-1944

Margaret **William**   Harry   Annie   Gilbert   Nellie   Sarah
                        Allison   Harrison   Elsie
Heversham Heversham Heversham Brathay   Brathay   Brathay   Brathay
1878-1966 1880-1921 1882-1975 1884-1971 1886-1958 1889-1985 1893-1976

** William Purdom (father) is referred to in the text as William Purdom senior. His son and subject of this book is referred to either as William or Purdom.

The place names indicate where they were born according to census records.

1

Cumbria and the Purdom Family

Cumbria, in the north west of England bordering Scotland, was created in 1974 from the former counties of Cumberland, Westmorland and that part of Lancashire to the north of Morecambe Bay. Today it attracts over seventeen million visitors every year to its glorious lakes and fells.

The intrepid Celia Fiennes (1662-1741) travelled widely through England and arrived in the north in the late 1690s. In Kendal one July she noted the greenness of the hills and absence of dense woodland; she feared the climate was too damp and cold to permit the cultivation of wheat, although barley, oats, peas and beans thrived. Having tasted the potted 'charr' (Arctic Char) of the lake, she was eager to visit Windermere, but found the lanes so narrow they would not accommodate a normal carriage. Pack horses and narrow carriages, like little wheelbarrows, being the usual forms of transport. The roads, such as they were, proved rough and crossing Kirkstone Pass on the way to Penrith, necessitated horses being reshod at regular intervals.

Arriving in Westmorland some 25 years later, Daniel Defoe described it as:

> a country eminent only for being the wildest, most barren and frightful of any that I have passed over in England… Bounded by a chain of mountains, which in the language of the country, are called Fells… Seeing nothing about me, in many places, but unpassable hills, whose tops, covered in with snow, seemed to tell us all the pleasant part of England was at an end.

William Wordsworth's book *A Guide through the District of the Lakes* was published in 1810. Typically he stressed the countryside could only appeal to people of taste; those worthy of appreciating its beauty. Having revealed the glories of the scenery, in 1844 he strenuously opposed the extension of the railway sending a sonnet 'On the projected Kendal and Windermere Railway' to national newspapers and the Prime Minister.

The *Morning Chronicle* was not sympathetic to his views, 'All that is beautiful in the Lake District belongs to the poet… no more incursions of the "common herd" must be made… let parks be made in the neighbourhood of Manchester.' Although the railway was built it was not allowed to go further than Windermere. But Rydal Mount (Wordsworth's home) was still not safe. By 1848 tourists were arriving in droves from Windermere station by carriage and omnibus to view the poet.

Despite its growing popularity in the nineteenth century, largely fostered by the Lakeland poets and the arrival of many wealthy northern industrialists who built their magnificent country retreats along the lake shores, the character of its people remained relatively unchanged.

The often harsh conditions bred resilience and independence in the inhabitants. According to Henry Swainson Cowper, the typical dalesmen had fair complexions and were strong but of spare build. Their manner was well-bred, their character reserved, and their independence extreme. To those who came to know them they were frank and open natured, but likely to drive a hard bargain. Although they were respectful to others, the older generation, in particular, were unlikely to 'Sir' their so called 'betters'. Swainson himself deplored touching his hat when meeting the squire as a regrettable innovation, because, he felt, it highlighted a distinction between the classes which had previously not existed.

At its best the relationship between squire and staff on an estate was one of mutual respect and benefit. Whilst both sides understood the constraints of the class divide, they could and did maintain friendly contact, sharing interests in local activities and parish responsibilities. This certainly seems to have been the

This photograph is believed to be Richard Purdom.

12

case for the Redmayne family of Brathay Hall and the Purdom family in its Lodge.

The Purdom family origins were long associated with the Scottish Borders, particularly Roxburghshire. Their family tradition had it they had once been Lairds of Purdom but it seems unlikely the Brathay branch of the family had such illustrious forbears.

Richard Purdom (William's grandfather) was born in Abbey Holme and his grandmother Margaret in Caldbeck. By 1851 they were living at Knott Place Cottage, Grasmere, with Richard described as an agricultural labourer. Richard's father David, also described as an agricultural labourer aged 60 was staying with them.

Their second son William (for the sake of clarity he is referred to as William senior) was born in 1851. During the next ten years Margaret had

William Purdom senior. Photograph courtesy of the Armitt Trust, Ambleside.

four more surviving children and doubtless accommodation was cramped. By 1861 David Purdom had joined over sixty other inmates in the Union Workhouse, Longtown, Carlisle.

The Harrison family had lived in the Langdales for many generations. In 1871 John Harrison was farming 94 acres at Busk, Little Langdale, together with wife Sarah and six children, aged between fifteen years and two months. Daughter Jane had already left to work as a kitchen maid in nearby Grasmere.

William senior, then a gardener in Burnley, married Jane Harrison, a servant aged

24, at Grasmere Church on 1st August 1877. The 1881 census shows William senior, as gardener to Captain Braithwaite at Plum Tree Hall, Heversham, near Kendal with wife Jane and two children Margaret aged three and William aged one.

At some time between the births of their second son Harry Allison in 1882 and daughter Annie in 1884, they moved from Heversham to their new home, the Lodge of Brathay Hall, near Ambleside. Three more children followed: Gilbert 1886, Nellie 1889 and Sarah Elsie in 1893.

The Lodge was comfortable and well-built; with three bedrooms, a fine sitting room, kitchen and veranda it would have been admired by many less fortunate locals. Across the road a trout pool, now called Brathay Dub, was once well known as Purdom's Pool.

Brathay Hall, set in 350 acres of park and woodland, with a private shoreline

The Lodge, Brathay Hall, photograph courtesy of Cumbria Archive Service.

on Lake Windermere was the home of Bond Street (London) draper Giles Redmayne; a genial character who liked to be rowed across the lake to Windermere, rather than take the road via Ambleside. He funded the building of Brathay Holy Trinity Church in 1836, on the site recommended by William Wordsworth.

Brathay Hall, photograph courtesy of the Brathay Trust.

The affection in which Giles Redmayne was held by local people was recorded on his death in April 1898:

> ...the death of Brathay's ever true, good, generous friend... when with sad hearts we laid our friend and benefactor in the little Churchyard he loved so well... may the thought that their (the family) sorrow is shared by all who knew their dear father lighten, if possible, their grief...

William senior, worked as head gardener at Brathay Hall for many years. He was an active member of the community: an enthusiastic cricketer in his younger days, a parish councillor and member of the Brathay Church choir.

Brathay Church was well supported and the hub of the small community. Its congregation gave generously to those in need from near and far. Talks and meetings were organised. One on behalf of the British Syrian Schools was recorded as being well attended while a Temperance Meeting was described as a distinct failure. However, the Temperance Movement was to gain support as the years passed. Drunkenness in towns and cities was rife; water often being undrinkable or a source of disease. Alcohol seemed the only way to achieve oblivion in times of crushing poverty. Both the Temperance League and Band of

Hope were regularly mentioned in the Brathay Church circular.

William senior, helped the ladies of the congregation to decorate the church and his efforts were particularly appreciated at Easter, Harvest Festival and Christmas when he worked alongside Miss Redmayne, whose family often provided flowers and fruit from the Brathay Hall gardens to add to the displays. The children would in their turn would be confirmed; on occasion help their father with the decorations (Harry and William) or take on bell ringing (Gilbert).

Christmas 1895 illustrates the importance of the church to the local community. 'Christmas has passed off very quietly and cheerfully in the little parish of Brathay. Nothing special occurred except in connection with the church.' As usual William senior, was responsible for the decorations 'and very pretty it looked.' On the two preceding Sundays, evening service was followed by carols sung by the Brathay Choir.

Brathay Church today

The annual children's dinner was held in the Brathay Sunday School at mid-day, followed by prize giving. A hearty meal for 90 was provided, apparently by the young people, but it is more than likely that their mothers were working hard in the background. Sunday School prizes won by the Purdom children included:

Boys Class 1   1st Harry;
                    2nd Gilbert
Girls Class I   1st Nellie
Girls Class 2   1st Annie

In the New Year it was the turn of the Young Men's Friendly Society to shine. On Tuesday, 21 January, they were commended for the success of the Concert held in Brathay

Schoolroom; a joint effort between the Young Men's Friendly Society and the local community. The room was packed. The entertainment consisted of singing and dialogues much to the delight of the audience. The duet *Sweet Voices* by Miss Redmayne and Margaret Purdom was 'listened to with rapt attention, and the audience would not be satisfied until it was repeated'. The dialogues produced roars of laughter, particularly *Paddy's Mistake* in which Willie Purdom featured as 'Miss Caughtim'. In the second half, the Rev. Milner's hunting song *We'll all go a hunting today* brought the house down. The concert ended with 'God save the Queen' and three cheers for the Young Men's Friendly Society and the ladies who had assisted in the entertainment (not forgetting Mrs Hartley who presided at the piano). A repeat performance took place on the following evening at Skelwith Bridge, the audience 'more than pleased with the evening's enjoyment.'

It is clear that William and Jane were determined to give their seven children the best possible start in life that they could afford. Education was the key and they went without themselves to provide this.

In late Victorian times the majority of working class children left school aged twelve or even younger to begin work and so contribute to the family income. It is not certain how many of the Purdom children attended the nearby school at Skelwith or for how long. William certainly went there for a time as he called himself an old scholar, when giving talks there in later years.

Skelwith was a rural school typical of its time with between 44 and 49 pupils attending during the 1890s. The school logbook records the efforts the teachers made to improve the rough speech of the children who 'almost uniformly ignore the aspirate.' The visits of the School Inspector were anticipated with some trepidation. On 12 May 1886 the Inspector's report commented on below average attendance; the children showing a most regrettable tendency to talk to with each other during the examination.

The pattern of the school year was regularly interrupted by family responsibilities. In July 1886 poor attendance was due to the start of hay-timing. Even as late as the 1960s children of farming families, in their last year at school and after examinations had finished, were allowed days off to help bring in the harvest. And worse was to come; on 22 April 1887 almost all of the boys disappeared in the afternoon to see the circus in Ambleside. What could be done to discourage this kind of thing? The girls were often called away and on 24 May 1889 attendance was described as simply wretched due to the demands of spring cleaning at home.

This might suggest that children of rural families had little encouragement or opportunity to progress. This was not the case for the schools in the Ambleside area. In 1891 the governors sent a letter to all parents saying that attendance would be free to all children. Books and all materials would be provided by the management but a nominal charge of 1d (old penny) per book would be made for the boys, and a half penny for the girls and nothing for the infants.

The three Purdom boys were enrolled at the Free Grammar School of Kelsick, in Ambleside; William on 28 June 1886 (his date of birth being recorded as 10 April 1879); Harry followed on 13 May 1889 aged seven and Gilbert on 21 May 1894 also aged seven.

At the end of the summer term marks were awarded for reading, recitation, essays, arithmetic and attendance. Success in these subjects was essential for those hoping to take the Scholarship Examinations.

Margaret went to St Mary's Girls National School in Ambleside. Here aged fifteen she started training as a pupil teacher, giving 'criticism lessons' on such exotic subjects as 'the turnip' (marked very satisfactory); 'avalanches and glaciers' and the 'Suez Canal' (considered of a high standard) and at the same time studying for formal teaching qualifications. By the beginning of 1897, having completed her pupil teacher apprenticeship, she was appointed as an Assistant teacher.

In June 1897 she gained a First Class Certificate in the Queen's Scholarship and was 'accepted at Whitelands', then situated in Chelsea and considered one of the leading women's teacher training colleges in the country; their aim was to produce a superior class of schoolmistress. Her absence from home was noticed.

William senior, was asked one day where his daughter was. When he explained that he and his wife had sent her to a well-known boarding school, he was informed that they had no business to send their daughter to such a school, as it was meant for the daughters of gentlemen, not for people like him and his wife. These words were remembered by her brother and were to influence his socialist leanings in later years.

William left school in 1894 and began his career in the gardening world, working under his father at Brathay Hall for some four years. At that time apprentice gardeners learned their trade as journeymen, starting with the most basic chores until they were judged knowledgeable enough to be trusted with specific tasks.

Aged eighteen he joined the soft wood propagating department at Stuart Low & Co of Enfield, a long established and respected nursery, specialising in rare and

William Purdom, aged 21, photograph © and courtesy of the
Lakeland Horticultural Society

unusual plants. About 40 years earlier Hugh Low had sailed to the East Indies to pursue his plant hunting activities, concentrating in particular on Borneo while his brother Stuart remained at home to develop the nursery.

Like many London nurseries in the 1880s the orchards were severely damaged by London smogs. Stuart decided it was essential to move to a more favourable site away from London and in 1883 bought sixteen acres of land at Bush Hill Park, Enfield, Middlesex. Here 33 glasshouses were eventually erected and fruit trees, roses and shrubs planted. Ten years later the nursery had expanded to some 60 acres and the specialist hardwood greenhouses were growing exotic specimens from Australia, including acacias.

At the turn of the century William moved to the prestigious Veitch Nurseries, at their Coombe Wood site in Kingston, Surrey, where he worked for nearly two years, again in the propagation department.

The Veitch family were leaders in the horticultural world. They had been involved in setting up the Royal Horticultural Society and the Chelsea Flower Show. Specializing in orchids and rare and unusual plants they commissioned men like William and Thomas Lobb to collect plants for them. In the 1840s and 1850s William Lobb travelled to North and South America from Panama through Chile to Patagonia, while Thomas explored the tropical rainforests of Malaysia.

In 1899 the Veitch family sponsored one of the greatest of all plant collectors – Ernest Wilson. He was to make several expeditions to China for them, sending back such a vast quantity of new and rare plants that between 1909 and 1913 Veitch Nurseries published a series of Chinese catalogues to promote the sale of their stock. Working in the propagating department at Coombe Wood, William would have seen many of these new introductions.

Back in Ambleside, Charles Henry Hough, FRCS, who had known William since childhood, had become his lifelong friend, champion and mentor. They both belonged to the Armitt Library in Ambleside. This remarkable library was founded in 1909 by the Armitt sisters, who were friends of Hough and known to William, who became one of the earliest Armitt members. The library operated on a subscription basis and specialised in works of local and scientific interest. It attracted the attention of the Wordsworths, Canon Rawnsley (a founder of the National Trust), Charlotte Mason and many more of the intellectual residents in the area. Through the sisters' connections the library received correspondence about Ambleside from social reformer Harriet Martineau; botanical drawings from Beatrix Potter, who had been a member since 1912; and an exceptional collection of photographic works by J. W. Brunskill, the Abraham Brothers, Herbert Bell, Moses Bowness and Charles Walmsley.

William senior, died on 12 September 1933. It was reported in the *Westmorland Gazette,* of 16 September:

> The death occurred early on Tuesday morning, after a long illness, of Mr William Purdom, Brathay Hall Lodge, at the age of 83 years. He was a native of Grasmere. He is survived by his wife, four sons, and two daughters. Mrs Purdom was before marriage Miss Harrison, Little Langdale. After being employed by Captain Braithwaite, Heversham, Mr Purdom came to Brathay Hall nearly 50 years ago as head gardener. For many years he was a member of the Brathay Church choir, and in his younger days he was an enthusiastic cricketer. Later he served on the parish council.*

His friends in Brathay remembered him and his family with affection:

> In Memoriam. On September 12th there passed from us one who was regarded with the greatest respect and affection by all. William Purdom lived a long life of faithful service. In his younger days he was an active worker in the church as chorister and in other ways. He has brought up a large family, all of them also rendering most useful service in their lives. They rise up and call him 'blessed'. May God grant him eternal rest and let light perpetual shine upon him, and may He grant consolation and strength to his bereaved relatives and friends, especially to her who has lovingly shared his life for 56 years! Jane died eleven years later aged 91.

Having spent two years with Veitch Nurseries, William was ready to extend his horticultural knowledge. His next move would be to Kew in 1902. He had already been away from home for almost five years. Although he would return for a brief period, his parents would not see him again after 1914.

---

* The entry is incorrect in that he was survived by four daughters and two sons not the reverse.

2
Kew

Being accepted by Kew was no mean achievement. Applicants had to be British, unmarried, aged 20 to 25, and with at least five years practical experience in horticulture, part of which had to have been under glass. Purdom was clearly ambitious and eager to learn. On 22 June 1902 he sent for an application form explaining he wished to have a period in the Royal Gardens, Kew, to increase his horticultural experience.

J. M. Abbott of Veitch's, who had known him since he was a schoolboy, sent a reference to William Watson (Kew Curator 1901-22), saying that Purdom was industrious and very much interested in his work; his steady character and honesty would ensure that Mr Watson would not regret giving him a trial.

In the 1890s the students at Kew followed an arduous schedule of over 54 hours a week. Even though the hours have changed, the mixture of work and study will be familiar to students of today. The day began at 6am with two hours work and a break of 45 minutes. This was followed twice a week by a period of 'botanising'; otherwise work continued until 6pm with an hour's break for lunch. Hourly lectures were given most evenings from 7pm and optional library studies were encouraged, finishing at 10pm.

In winter they worked from dawn to dusk and in later years were allowed some Saturday afternoons off. At the time Purdom joined Kew the wages were 21s (shillings) per week – barely enough to cover living expenses.

In addition to their horticultural work, students were expected to attend a hundred one hour long lectures covering economics; geographic, structural and systemic botany; plus physics and chemistry during their two year's training. By the end of the working day they were often exhausted and enthusiasm for the lectures at a low.

Although the extra time spent in the library was optional, a record was kept of all the lectures attended and was included with the final leaving certificate. This would enable prospective employers to see whether a candidate had a habit of missing lectures and so possibly lack the dedication necessary to progress in a responsible position. A good report from Kew opened up many opportunities for student gardeners. Most of them came from relatively humble origins, but with success, they could gain employment on prestigious estates or in botanical gardens overseas.

The Director of Kew at this time was Sir William Thiselton-Dyer, dedicated to the improvement of the gardens and a strict disciplinarian. He was known to be insistent on correct standards of dress. One member of staff had been dismissed for coming to work in a bowler hat, after being warned that only foremen were allowed to wear them in the garden. The arrival of three female gardeners was not entirely welcome either; Thiselton-Dyer apparently insisted they should wear knickerbockers and caps to make themselves as unattractive as possible. The knickerbockers both delighted and shocked local residents and had to be covered by long coats on their journeys to and from the gardens.

Purdom's early years at Kew seemed to go well. He attended the annual dinner at the end of each May and became a member of the Mutual Improvement Society, which had been founded in 1871 by Sir Joseph Hooker. Its aim was to encourage student members to share their horticultural interests by giving talks on Monday evenings from September to April. In early March 1904 he shared a demonstration on pruning and propagation with William Dallimore (who was to become one of Kew's greatest experts on trees and shrubs). On 1st April he was promoted to sub-foreman in the arboretum and in 1905 was awarded the Sir Joseph Hooker prize, for the best speaker or contributor to the Mutual Improvement Society.

On 4 November 1905 Purdom was dismissed for 'agitating'. So what happened in those few months, to turn an honest and industrious young man into a trouble maker? Concerns over poor wages and long working hours had been raised as early as 1891. In 1905 foremen, student gardeners and labourers asked that improvements to their working conditions be considered and in February formed the Kew Employees Union (a branch of the United Government Workers Federation) and elected Purdom as their Secretary.

Purdom was by conviction a Liberal and felt strongly about the rights of the working man. Through his socialist interests he knew a number of Labour Members of Parliament which was to prove particularly useful in the months ahead. He had no hesitation in submitting a petition to the Board of Agriculture on behalf of the Union members. This was received by Thiselton-Dyer, via the curator.

It could not have fallen on more unsympathetic ears. Even the writing of such a 'memorial' inflamed Thistelton-Dyer who refused to receive or forward it to the Board of Agriculture, saying that he would 'not recognise any body which comes between me and my staff'. He commented further that he viewed Purdom's communication as a breach of discipline.

The feelings of dissatisfaction grew. After work on Sunday evening 3 November a public meeting was called on Kew Green, addressed by Labour MPs, the Government Workers' Federation, with Purdom and the Chairman of the Employees' Union representing the discontented staff. On the Monday morning both were immediately sacked by Thistelton-Dyer.

This was a sensitive period for the country as a whole with union unrest becoming more widespread and a General Election due on 13 January. It was felt by Kew authorities that any confrontation at this time would be inadvisable and only provide ammunition for Labour sympathisers. This conclusion was reinforced by the intervention of some MPs and representatives of the United Government Workers Federation on behalf of the two dismissed men.

Two MPs supported Purdom. Firstly Thomas Summerbell, Sunderland's first Labour MP, who was elected in 1906. He set up his printing business in Sunderland and was elected to the town council in 1892. Son of a coal trimmer, he was particularly concerned about the plight of the labouring classes, the education of the poor and the consequences of unemployment. He travelled throughout the country in 1907 to promote the values of socialism.

His second supporter was Will

Thomas Summerbell, MP,
courtesy of Local Studies, Sunderland City Council.

Crooks who spent his early years in the Poplar workhouse which influenced him deeply. In 1900 he became the first Labour mayor of Poplar. His unexpected victory, over the Conservative candidate, in the 1902 election, made him the fourth Labour MP. He campaigned tirelessly against poverty and inequality until his death in 1921. Thousands attended his funeral which was filmed for British Pathe newsreel.

Thiselton-Dyer was ordered to back down and the two men were reinstated on 13 November. He found himself in a situation he could not understand; his authority had been questioned and he realised his status amongst the gardening staff had been weakened. His loyalty to Kew was never in question but he realised it was time to go. He resigned in December and was replaced by Lieut. Col. David Prain.

Vanity Fair caricature of Will Crooks, MP, by 'Spy' (Leslie Ward), 6 April 1905, entitled 'The Labourer is worthy of his hire'.

Prain found himself in an unenviable position; not only having to re-establish a degree of discipline but inheriting the consequences of a major omission on the application form for the 1905 student intake. A rather easy going attitude had developed towards the two year student programme, at the end of which students normally left to take on permanent employment.

The failure to mention the two year cut off formally on the application form led students to believe they could continue working at Kew. This had never had been the case either at Kew or any other botanical gardens. Logically if no students left there could be no vacancies for a new intake. Prain made it clear that a mistake had been made and, in line with normal procedure, the students would have to leave in 1907.

Once Purdom was promoted to the position of sub-foreman in the Kew Arboretum, he assumed that he was now a member of the permanent staff. Apparently the technical term was 'non-established' staff, indicating the position was of limited duration. He was regarded as an excellent gardener, a very good propagator and one who would stand up for his staff, provided they did not neglect their work.

William Dallimore commented that 1906/7 were particularly difficult years. He felt the continuing dissatisfaction and unrest amongst students and gardeners was being encouraged by outside political activists for their own ends. The 3 November 1907 issue of *The Gardeners' Chronicle* reported on a meeting between the Kew Employees' Union (represented by Purdom), the United Government Workers Federation and Earl Carrington, President of the Board of Agriculture and Fisheries. Earl Carrington promised the employment issues at Kew would be considered carefully.

The question of wages had still not been settled and the long working hours remained an issue. The gardeners said they would not attend lectures until the working week was reduced from the current 54 hours. They failed to understand the impact this stance might have on future employers, who would view with dismay their demands for more money and a shorter working day. Many employers were now convinced the men had absorbed revolutionary ideas and in fact had little to complain about. The dispute also discouraged potential applicants from joining the scheme.

Kew became a hotbed of rumours and misunderstandings. Prain insisted the two year limit must be stated clearly at the time of admission and added that this should apply to sub-foremen too. This was to have a major impact on Purdom.

Prain tried to balance the needs of Kew, while acting in a fair manner towards the students. He made it clear no student from the 1905 intake would be expected to leave without having found suitable employment and that there was absolutely no question of them being dismissed, as this would be a black mark on any job application.

This stance was confirmed on 30 December 30 1907:

The Board of Agriculture permits the retention, till 31 March, 1908, of any young gardener now at Kew whose term of service may have ended prior to that date but who may not prior to that date have secured a new situation.

The Board have also sanctioned the retention for a 4th year of the services of Mr William Purdom as a sub-foreman, and owing to the fact that the 4th year of Mr Purdom's service as a sub-foreman has already commenced the board have ruled that the final year of his service is to be held as commencing 24 December 1907.

Purdom seems to have been persuaded by his political friends to challenge the Board's decision by acting as a test case and not applying for employment. Dallimore feared that in his determination to support others, Purdom failed to realise he was being manipulated by outside activists, who promised to stand by him throughout and evidently did not.

A telegram sent on 4 March 1908 advised Prain that MP Thomas Summerbell was about to raise the plight of the ten Kew gardeners 'under notice to leave' in a question in the House of Commons to the representative of the Board of Agriculture, Sir Edward Strachey. Was Kew intending to 'turn off these men without employment?'

Six months later Thomas Summerbell appealed to Sir Edward Strachey specifically on behalf of Purdom, to allow him yet more time to find a suitable position. To make the situation absolutely clear, on 2 November Prain wrote a twelve page letter to the Board of Agriculture, detailing why it was impossible to extend Purdom's employment beyond Christmas Eve.

He explained he had made every effort to use considerable tact and patience in dealing with the gardeners' complaints. For over two years he had been subjected to an attitude of studied disrespect, but felt that by acting reasonably he would eventually be able to regain their confidence. When alone a student might be polite, but when two or three were working together his 'existence was still ostentatiously ignored'.

He simply could not consider allowing Purdom to remain at Kew in any capacity, as this would suggest that the management simply did not dare ask him to leave and that agitation, in whatever form, worked. This would result in it being impossible to maintain any kind of discipline amongst the current staff in the future.

In spite of these comments, Prain acknowledged that Purdom was a good workman but that he feared his involvement in the student unrest and his 'singular capacity for misinterpreting the bearing of facts' had damaged his prospects for future employment. He had to leave Kew on 24 December 1908. There would be no further negotiation.

In fact Purdom had already received an exceptional offer from C. S. Sargent of the Arnold Arboretum, Massachusetts, USA, at a wage of £180 a year, plus accommodation and the prospect of an increase to £400. This position might offer entire charge of the arboretum in due course to a suitable applicant.

Prain explained his position as being one of extreme delicacy when it came to handling Purdom, who 'made it necessary for me to do what lay in my power to assist him without him being aware of the fact lest, from mistaken pride or for some other reason he should decline to accept any situation so offered to him'.

Purdom did turn down the offer, leaving Sargent with the impression that he was not very enterprising and unwilling to take even the slightest risk. Prain felt it highly unlikely that Purdom would ever consider a permanent position at Kew, with a starting salary of just £104.

The situation remained uncertain throughout November as Purdom failed to make any formal application to the Kew Board to join the permanent staff. Finally, at the beginning of December he wrote directly to Earl Carrington, President of the Board of Agriculture. His letter outlined the importance of the work he did as sub-foreman and again raised the fact that the rules of tenure had changed after he took up the position. In his support, the Liberal MP for Brentford, Dr V. H. Rutherford contacted Earl Carrington, asking him to reconsider Purdom's position, saying he knew him as 'a good, honest, go-ahead fellow'.

Yet again Prain was asked for his views. In a six page letter of 6 December he ends by saying the Purdom issue now threatened the future of Kew:

> If the request made by Mr Purdom be refused it will be possible to ensure that the Royal Gardens at Kew shall continue to be, as they have been for one hundred and fifty years, a training ground whence young gardeners can be drafted to fill with credit the more important horticultural posts throughout the colonies and dependencies of Britain. If this request be granted the whole position is abandoned... [and] necessarily involves the destruction of Kew as an institution of public utility.

When advised that the Earl had no intention of cancelling the decision, Purdom's response is another letter 'respectfully pointing out that as a Government servant' he had every right to approach the Earl directly; it makes for uncomfortable reading and might have been drafted by his erstwhile union friends.

A final letter from Prain was sent to the curator, with a copy posted to Purdom at 4.45 pm on Christmas Eve, 'I am to inform you that my instructions on the subject are clear and Mr Purdom's engagement must terminate this afternoon.'

Purdom did not leave Kew under a complete cloud. His colleagues in the Kew Union had publicly presented him with a watch and chain and fountain pens. But their report in the 1909 issue of *The Kew Guild* had one final sting in the tail saying that his 'services to the Gardens during the 6¼ years he was employed were such as to entitle him to a place on the permanent staff.'

Although his colleagues in the Kew Union knew of his plans, it seems that Purdom had by now distanced himself from the outside activists as indicated in a letter written by James G. King of the United Government Workers' Federation on 14 February 1909 to Earl Carrington. The letter was entitled 'Protest from the United Government Workers' Federation against the discharge of Wm. Purdom.'

Seemingly unaware that Purdom now had a position, the United Government Workers' Federation also published an extraordinary article which then appeared in the *Richmond and Twickenham Times* on 13 February under the heading 'The Case of Mr Purdom'

The Case of Mr. Purdom.

Under the title "Brains Not Wanted," the "Government Workers' Advocate" refers to the recent discharge of Mr. W. Purdom from Kew Gardens. The journal says:—

Ever since Purdom sought to organise the staff for mutual protection and improvement he has been a marked man; summary dismissal was the first evidence of official displeasure, and when this outrage had to be rectified other means were adopted, until at last the time limit was invoked to get rid of him. He had not been engaged under any time-limit arrangement—but that is a small matter where Government officials are concerned. Breach of faith or of contract are never allowed to stand in the way of their desires, however explicit they may have been; and when Earl Carrington was appealed to he simply upheld his officials, with th'a proviso—that Purdom should not be discharged until he had other employment to go to. But even this promise could not be kept, for no sooner had the Parliamentary session closed, and the heads of departments gone away on their holidays, than the official malevolence showed its cruel head, and on Christmas Eve Purdom is informed by letter that his services will be no longer required. From the moment he sought to improve the conditions of employment at Kew his footsteps have been dogged by official opposition and vindictiveness.

Courtesy the London Borough of Richmond on Thames, Leisure Services.

Under the title 'Brains Not Wanted' the 'Government Workers' Advocate' refers to the recent discharge of Mr W. Purdom from Kew Gardens. *The Journal* says:

Ever since Purdom sought to organise the staff for mutual protection and improvement he has been a marked man; summary dismissal was the first evidence of official displeasure, and when this outrage had to be rectified other means were adopted until at last the time limit was invoked to get rid of him. He had not been engaged under any time-limit arrangement – but, that is a small

William Purdom when at Kew, courtesy of The Journal of the Kew Guild.

matter where Government officials are concerned. Breach of faith or of contract are never allowed to stand in the way of their desires, however explicit they may have been; and when Earl Carrington was appealed to he simply upheld his officials, with the proviso – that Purdom should not be discharged until he had other employment to go to. But even this promise was not kept, for no sooner had the Parliamentary session closed, and the heads of deparments gone away on their holidays, than the official malevolence showed its cruel head, and on Christmas Eve Purdom is informed by letter that his services will be longer required. From the moment he sought to improve the conditions of employment at Kew his footsteps have been dogged by official opposition and vindictiveness.

The folly of discharging men of ability and competence must be evident to all who have the maintenance of Kew as a national Establishment at heart. To leave these splendid collections of plants to the care of novices is an act of sheer idiocy; public money has been very lavishly expended upon them, and we contend that a competent staff of gardeners should be maintained to look after them. The training of young men should be under the direction of men of experience and ability, and not left, as at present, to the haphazard method of finding out what they can while doing all the work - not for wages, but on a bare subsistence allowance. This expert staff should be selected and recruited from the most promising and efficient men who can be secured, to whom should be open the highest positions in the establishment as they become vacant. The position of curator, director and assistant director should be the prizes for ability and efficiency; the men would then have some incentive to work and to study, and the public would benefit by having the best value for money spent.

Its impact on Purdom, if there were any, could only have been negligible. He had already left England for America, on 3 February to take up his new appointment as plant collector in China.

3

Becoming a Plant Collector

During that last fraught year at Kew, Purdom must have worried about the future. His training and undoubted skills should have ensured him a prestigious position. Kew students were in demand at home and abroad, but however glowing the references from his past employers or managers at Kew, he could only be regarded as a risk; someone who might challenge the authority of any new master. Even in later years Reginald Farrer would comment on his inability to 'bend the knee'.

It seems extraordinary that Purdom left Kew on Christmas Eve 1908 and within barely five weeks was on his way to China. In fact David Prain had kept true to his promise to act for Purdom but to keep his interventions discrete.

As early as February 1908 Harry Veitch and Charles Sprague Sargent of the Arnold Arboretum, Massachusetts, had been discussing joint sponsorship of a plant collecting expedition to northern China. The successes of the two great plant collectors Ernest Wilson and George Forrest in the southern provinces of Szechuan and Yunnan had been spectacular.

Harry Veitch, courtesy of Caradoc Doy.

Sargent was convinced that an expedition to the northern provinces of Shensi and Kansu would yield new hardy plants and trees, particularly from the mountainous forest regions.

Veitch clearly had some reservations as to the expense and bad timing of such an enterprise but Sargent reassured him that the arrangements would take time and circumstances could improve. Besides which the botanical treasures of China would prove a commercial success. The problem was to find 'a good man'.

Sargent had considered Purdom as an assistant superintendent of the Arnold Arboretum but Purdom had not been enthusiastic. He then asked Prain to encourage Purdom to reconsider and explain that this position would be far more

Charles Sprague Sargent,
© President and Fellows of Harvard College,
Arnold Arboretum Archives.

rewarding than anything he was likely to find in Britain. The offer was made at the time when relations between Purdom and Kew management were deteriorating rapidly.

Sargent wrote to Prain saying that Forrest had turned down the opportunity to go to northern China. However, he felt that the expedition should not be abandoned as the expenses were going to be shared with Veitch. He wondered if Purdom would be suitable but perhaps lacked the necessary enterprise and grit. There could be no doubt as to his intelligence and knowledge of plants, particularly trees.

At the same time Harry Veitch had gone to Kew to discuss the project with Prain and the curator (Watson). Both thought that Purdom would be a good candidate, if he could be persuaded to go, and would be a better choice than Forrest who was considered to be a little difficult. Veitch felt that the younger generation were a peculiar lot and seemingly difficult to please. Nevertheless he arranged to meet Purdom to discuss the outlines of the two to three year expedition, which offered a salary of £200 a year and a bonus, if successful; plus £400 for travelling expenses.

Purdom had no experience of travelling and no knowledge of Chinese; but Forrest would also have had language problems since the dialect in the north was quite different from Yunnan.

Veitch's offer took Purdom by surprise. Although he was interested in reading about collectors and had handled seeds from Wilson's expeditions at Kew and had seen the plants Wilson sent to Veitch while working at Coombe Wood, he had never thought of becoming a collector himself. Understandably he needed time to think. He said how unhappy he still was at being given notice to leave Kew, but must have put this complaint in such a way that it did not worry Veitch.

Veitch found him bright and intelligent and temperamentally suited to become a good collector. Of course, there could be no hope of finding a second Wilson, but Purdom seemed more likely to follow their instructions than Forrest.

On 31 December 1908 Prain wrote to Sargent saying how pleased he was to learn of the offer to Purdom. 'We here have the highest opinion of his intelligence and of his knowledge of plants and the opinion of his friends has always been that he was a pushing, energetic young man.' It is almost possible to hear the relief in this letter. Now there was a chance that Purdom could leave with honour being maintained on both sides and China was so splendidly far away.

Having agreed to accept this remarkable and unexpected offer on 8 January 1909, Purdom would have found the next three weeks passed in a blizzard of information.

William Watson, Kew curator, had given a very satisfactory report about Purdom to Veitch, as had William Dallimore. Both spoke of his energy in undertaking any task ('if anything too energetic' said Watson) and Dallimore, as his foreman, had confirmed that he was a naturally amiable man and that his only fault was to have become mixed up with politics. Sargent, however, wanted him to visit America for a final personal interview.

In the meantime, essential letters of introduction were obtained with Prain's help from the Foreign Office; the British Minister in Peking; Sir Alexander Hosie, Commercial Attaché to Peking; Colonel Anderson of the British Legation Guard, Peking; the China Inland Mission and various banks in Peking and Tientsin, regarding the payment of his salary, thanks to the support of Messrs Rothschild.

Practical advice was elicited from Sir Robert Hart, a British diplomat in China. There was also the question as to the payment of his salary. Would Sargent arrange this or should it be handled by Purdom's elder sister Margaret, since she was already working in London as a school teacher?

The key issues were to familiarise Purdom thoroughly with the Chinese plants from Wilson's herbarium collection and those from his expeditions growing at Veitch's Coombe Wood Nursery. He also needed to see the numerous Chinese specimens collected by Dr Augustine Henry who was based in Cambridge. Dr Henry gave exceptionally helpful advice about the route Purdom might follow, especially in the Wutai mountains of Shansi, as this was a virtually unexplored district. He advised against going north of Peking.

There was also the matter of learning how to use the camera. Mr Wallis of Kew had previously trained Wilson and would do the same for Purdom. Later Purdom would complain about the difficulties of handling glass plates. Veitch had mentioned the possibility of a Kodak and films. Veitch had also undertaken to equip Purdom with all the necessaries, including books and maps, and had arranged for everything, except what was needed for immediate travelling, to be sent direct to Tientsin. This arrangement was changed a few days later to Shanghai. He told Sargent that he was becoming more pleased with Purdom the more he saw of him.

Purdom was particularly happy to hear he would meet Ernest Wilson in Shanghai and also his great friend, an ex-Kewite, MacGregor who was supervisor to the Shanghai Public Parks and Gardens. On 19 January Purdom travelled home to take leave of his friends and parents. He had to be back in London by 27 January.

Having asked to see Purdom personally, it seems Sargent changed his mind. However, Veitch had already booked the tickets and at this late stage changing arrangements would be difficult, especially obtaining a refund on the £11 paid for crossing the Atlantic. So on Wednesday, 3 February, Purdom set sail on the *Oceanic* from Southampton, bound for New York. Veitch was concerned about the crossing as it was blowing hard when he left. He asked Sargent to tell him that everyone was thinking about him and wondering how he was getting on.

Purdom now had two masters, each with different expectations. Veitch throughout displayed a more sympathetic and caring attitude towards Purdom's welfare. Sargent, however, was a different character and sympathy or understanding were not words likely to appear often in his vocabulary. Coming from a family of Boston 'Brahmins' who lived almost like nobility; exercising authority came naturally to him. He could be haughty and tactless yet had superb administrative skills. The dedication and discipline he expected of himself and others were very like those of Thistelton-Dyer at Kew. He effectively created the Arnold Arboretum.

Sargent had chosen the location – obstinately so – and had given no regard to the fact that previous explorers had found little to commend any plant collector to the harsh areas of northern China.

During the stormy voyage to America Purdom no doubt had the opportunity to re-read Veitch's simple outline brief. The expedition would take two to three years; location northern China; object to collect seeds or plants of trees, including conifers and any plants that had a commercial value such as lilies, primulas or other hardy herbaceous novelties. He had to be quite clear that everything (herbarium samples, seeds and photographs) would belong to Sargent or Veitch, unless he was told otherwise. The only exception being one set of herbarium specimens he might keep for himself – there is no evidence he did so.

Sargent's brief proved an entirely different matter, extending in extraordinary detail over some eight pages.

As early as possible in spring he should set out northwards from Peking (Chihli) to the Imperial Hunting Grounds beyond the Great Wall. A special passport would have to be obtained. The prospects in the area did not seem promising as they had not been covered by any other botanist. In August he should return to Peking and set out for Wutai-shan, a sacred mountain in Shansi (a province of 60,000 square miles, so in area larger than England and Wales put together). Reports had it that there were four or five species of *Picea* and possibly two of *Larix* that dropped their seeds in September. After which he must make a hasty return to the Imperial Hunting Grounds to collect seed and make autumn herbarium samples of those plants he had discovered in spring.

The next year should be concentrated in Shensi. Somewhere there was an area unexplored by any European botanist and a mountain called *Moutan-shan*, between 35° and 36° where the tree peony could be found. The third season would be in Kansu. Obviously it might be difficult to cover the whole area in the time available.

Sargent considered that woody plants were of prime importance. Purdom must make six sets of herbarium samples to illustrate the different areas in which a particular specimen grew; two or three sets would be adequate for herbaceous plants. In addition he should prepare a set of Chinese ferns and a separate set of all terrestrial orchids and aconites.

Seeds of ALL woody plants had to be collected, not in great quantity, just sufficient to raise 500-600 specimens each of the most valuable. Where propagation by seed was not likely to succeed then grafts or cuttings had to be taken and packed in sphagnum moss and mailed as soon as possible – always assuming there was a mail service available. Herbaceous seeds and bulbs (surrounded in clay) were to be sent direct to Veitch in London in the bags provided. Samples of nuts, in variety, should be acquired from local markets and also edible grains.

Photographs (including bark, flower and fruit) were to be taken of any trees Purdom could not identity and cross referenced to the herbarium specimen; also studies were required of the scenery and local people.

Sargent did not expect long or numerous reports to be sent (but later complained when they were not) but keeping a daily journal of activities and discoveries was essential. He was also instructed to keep detailed notes of all expenditure and to post a statement every six months. Sadly Purdom lost many of his photographic plates and precious field notes either in dangerous river crossings or when under attack by bandits.

It was fortunate that inexperienced Purdom was chosen to cope with this flood of demands. Forrest had been called difficult and was far more likely, as a straight talking Scot, who did not tolerate fools gladly, to have said exactly what he thought about 'send by mail… if it exists in the interior'.

As Veitch said, no plant collector had been better prepared. Sargent's detailed programme made it clear what was required; supplies had been purchased and shipped out in advance; letters of introduction obtained and advice asked of one of the greatest plant collectors.

Ernest Wilson's reaction to Purdom being chosen was complex. Of a far more outgoing and sociable character than Forrest he was nonetheless slightly put out to hear about Purdom. He had been in China collecting for Veitch for some years and had not yet seen his two and a half year old daughter. He freely admitted his wife would have been desperately upset if he had stayed away from home any longer. On the other hand, it would have been gratifying to have been asked or at least given some word of warning. Having said that, Wilson assured Sargent that he would give Purdom all the help and advice he could when and if they managed to meet in Shanghai. He hoped Purdom would be more receptive to his suggestions than the American collector Frank Meyer, whom he had tried to help previously.

4

China and the End of Empires

What did Purdom know about China? *The Land of the Lamas*, published in 1891 by William Woodville Rockhill, an American diplomatist, whom he was to meet in Peking, gave some details of the route he was to follow through Shansi, Shensi and Kansu and the peoples and customs he would meet there, but political information was lacking.

The golden Edwardian years were indeed a paradox. For the wealthy, leisure and the opportunity to travel and enjoy life had never been greater. The lower classes, however, were still trapped in a Victorian age of service and often grinding poverty. Few, if any, could see a way to improve their lot. Many realised they had the ability to achieve more but simply could not find the means to do so.

Purdom had already experienced the rise of socialist ideals at home. In China he would see the gulf between rich and poor on a magnified scale, not only from the Chinese point of view but also through the attitudes of privileged Westerners. Different cultures were considered to be inferior despite their long history and exquisite art. The latter should be obtained as easily and cheaply as possible.

The First World War claimed the lives of millions and transformed the social structure of a continent. Empires fell and monarchs were assassinated. In China the ruling Manchu dynasty was toppled but the dreams of an open and democratic republic did not quite materialise. Communism would eventually rebuild those walls that the West thought it had successfully breached.

The China to which Purdom was to travel in 1909 was in turmoil; dangerous not only to the wide eyed foreigners but to the entire population from peasant to the last Emperor of the Manchu Dynasty.

The Manchus had seized power in Northern China in the middle of the seventeenth century. Eventually they ruled the whole country and seemed completely opposed to change. Their China was the Middle Kingdom, the centre of the earth. At the turn of the twentieth century the Royal Court in the Forbidden City still operated on feudal lines and all that lay beyond it was alien and suspect.

Few Emperors would have known anything about the daily lives of their subjects in Peking.

Merchants and politicians from the West were viewed with particular suspicion. Wherever they went their only purpose was to seize other people's lands; change Chinese beliefs through missionary activity and make commercial profit by any means available. In order to understand this attitude it is helpful to look at the Opium Wars of 1839-42 and 1856-60.

China was seen as ripe for development of so called free trade and opium was to be the key that brought it to the mercy of the West. The East India Company had access to opium and by manipulating the terms of trading agreements with China, exchanged it for silver, tea and other commodities; at first only in modest amounts, then as the addiction grew, by the shipload. The Chinese authorities tried to stamp out the habit by making the smoking of opium illegal, but the trade simply went underground. Although opium was not new to China (it had been used medicinally for hundreds of years) its escalating use alarmed the government. Lin Tse-Hsu* was the Chinese Commissioner in Canton and his actions precipitated the first Opium War. He ordered the destruction of all opium stock held at the docks and in the warehouses. Reparations would be required.

In 1839 he wrote to Queen Victoria (a letter she apparently did not receive):

Yet there are barbarian ships that strive to come here for trade for the purpose of making a great profit. The wealth of China is used to profit the barbarians. That is to say, the great profit made by barbarians is all taken from the rightful share of China. By what right do they then in return use the poisonous drug to injure the Chinese people? Even though the barbarians may not necessarily intend to do us harm, yet in coveting profit to an extreme, they have no regard for injuring others...

I have heard that the smoking of opium is very strictly forbidden by your country; that is because the harm caused by opium is clearly understood. Since it is not permitted to do harm to your own country, then even less should you let it be passed on to the harm of other countries – how much less to China!

The Western powers might well have thought they were opening up China to new trading opportunities and they were prepared to reinforce this policy by force and did so.

---

* Also seen as Lin Zexu or Lin Zixu.

The cartoon below appeared in the French satirical magazine *Le Charivari* in 1840 and was translated into a variety of languages. The caption is translated from the original.

By 1842, the Chinese were obliged to reinstate the opium trade. Other western

"I say you must buy this poison immediately. We want you to really poison yourselves so that we can have plenty of tea to digest our beefsteaks."

nations were also becoming involved. The settlement would increase trade and missionary involvement in China. Hostilities broke out again and yet more concessions were required. The Second Opium War 1856-60 saw demands for the legalisation of the opium trade, freedom of missionary activity and the right of foreigners to reside in Peking; all were finally accepted.

By the late nineteenth century China was in the hands of the Empress Dowager Tzu-hsi (Cixi) known to the Chinese as 'the old or venerable Buddha'. Two factions emerged at the court; one committed to the old ways and the other trying to learn from the industrialised west. Corruption was rife. The Forbidden City was a seething mass of intrigue and conspiracy.

In an attempt to rid the country of the hated foreigners, Empress Tzu-hsi encouraged the Boxers to demonstrate their support of the Manchu dynasty. They believed that the decorations they wore gave them supernatural protection against the bullets of the Europeans. By June 1900 the foreign Legations in Peking were under siege. It was nearly two months before 20,000 troops left Tsientsin in a race to rescue the besieged foreigners.

With defeat imminent, Dowager Empress Tzu-hsi escaped from Peking in disguise and the city was eventually partitioned by the different Western powers. The looting and destruction which followed were shameful; even missionaries, diplomats and their wives joined in.

During this time she relied on the support of Yuan Shih-k'ai and his army. She eventually disowned the Boxers and returned to Peking. As 1908 drew to a close she knew her health was failing. Her main objectives were to retain power for as long as possible and appoint a worthy heir.

Whether she arranged the death of Prince Kuang-hsu is uncertain. Many of the rumours circulated about the Empress can be attributed to the fabrications in books such as those written by Edmund Backhouse. Legend had it that with his last remaining breath Prince Kuang-hsu cursed Tzu-hsi, who had made him Emperor but killed his favourite concubine. If the legend is true then the curse worked as she died on the following day 15 November 1908, having named the baby Pu Yi, son of Prince Chun the Second, as her successor. It is said that both the Emperor and Dowager Empress showed signs of arsenic poisoning.

During the remaining years of the Manchu Dynasty the government proved weak and corrupt. The Emperor was far too young to exercise any real power and was totally unaware of life outside the Forbidden City. Factions arose, warlords and bandits terrorised the country. The thousands of eunuchs, former royal wives

The Qing Dynasty Dowager Empress of China, Tzu-hsi, by Yu Xunling, 1900, Smithsonian Institute.

and concubines continued their exorbitant spending; draining the imperial treasury in the process.

In February 1912 the Last Emperor Pu Yi abdicated and a month later Yuan Shih-k'ai, former general and leader of his own private army, who had supported Tzu-hsi in her later years, became President of the Republic of China. Peace was still not to come. Opposition arose against his dictatorial rule and administration. Not satisfied with his position as President Yuan announced he would restore the monarchy with himself as Emperor but died in 1916, deserted by his former supporters.

Yuan Shih-k'ai, Rio DeSieux, circa 1915.*

* Reference in chapter of *Current History,* Vol. 3, page 380, *New York Times.*

5

The First Expedition 1909-1912

To undertake any expedition into unknown regions, even today, is an awesome task. Purdom set out alone, without the benefits of modern communications. In this he was no different from any other plant collector of the time. However, his resources were limited and he was sent to the harsher northern provinces of Inner Mongolia, Shensi, Shansi, Kansu and the borderlands of Tibet.

Having spent as much time in Boston as Sargent would allow, he left by train in mid-February 1909 for Vancouver and the ocean crossing to Shanghai. Until mid-ocean it was a rough passage but the second part of the journey in calm seas proved very pleasant. It took about a month to reach Shanghai as the ship called at various ports, including those in Japan, where the passengers were allowed to disembark but had little time to travel far into the interior.

About the third week in March 1909, Purdom arrived in Shanghai, where he was able to spend a few days with his Kew colleague MacGregor, who was in charge of the local parks. He also met Ernest Wilson who was in good spirits and gave him invaluable advice, not least on the complexities of foreign exchange rates and made him a loan until he could visit a bank in Peking.

On Saturday 27 March he boarded the SS *Shuntien* bound for the northern port of Tientsin, where a few days later he met Sir Alexander Hosie, the acting Commercial Attaché. In Peking, he presented his letters of introduction to Mr Rockhill, American Ambassador to China, and Sir John Jordan, British Envoy to China.

He stayed at the famous Grand Hotel des Wagons-Lits, a favourite of foreign visitors; an imposing building close to the station and in the centre of the Legation district. For some, arrival at the hotel was a culture shock; a Parisian style entrance set with green wicker chairs and small tables and full of European ladies and gentlemen. Individual rooms had an English style bed, silk eiderdown, electric light, easy chair and hot and cold water. Through the lace curtains workmen and rickshaws could be seen in the crowded streets below.

At that time the hotel was run by an Austrian and according to one visitor that meant the food tended to be rather Germanic in style. Purdom was fortunate to have arrived at the end of the month and so avoided one of the many dust storms, frequent at that time of year. These storms resembled London smogs as the sun disappeared. A blizzard of choking red dust made it almost impossible to breathe. Windows in the hotel were closed and few people went out, but the interior was still covered in inches of dust.

Although Purdom had lived in London for over five years, he found Peking crowded and exceptionally expensive. This was largely due to the impending funeral of the Emperor, Prince Kuang-hsu, whose body had been lying in state, together with that of the Dowager Empress, on Coal Hill inside the Forbidden City, since their deaths the previous November.

The mourning arrangements were precise and far reaching: men could not shave their heads for one hundred days; no red clothes could be worn (except by children); all red signs were covered in white or blue; no weddings could take place for three months and Manchus were forbidden to marry for three years. The

View over Peking from the Great Wall by William Purdom.
© The Royal Geographic Society

mourning restrictions were lifted for one day only when the new Emperor, Pu Yi aged three, was carried to the dragon throne by the Prince Regent.

It would be almost a month before Purdom could obtain the necessary Chinese passports to travel into the interior. All official administration had been put on hold until the funeral was over. It was an impressive affair, with white camels and horses in a cortege which took the whole day to pass through the city. Foreigners felt it necessary to act with sensitivity and respect.

Time passed swiftly as he organised mules, carts, stores and hiring Chinese 'boys' willing to undertake the journey with him. He made careful notes of any interesting trees around Peking, including willows, poplars, chestnuts and cherries in particular. Identification was difficult, it being early in the year before leaves were fully open. A beautiful anemone, most suitable for a rockery, took his eye and he sent samples to Harry Veitch as an experiment with the postal system, commenting if the plant did not survive the journey he would send roots (the best method of propagation) in the autumn.

With the help of Colonel Anderson of the Legation Guard, a stalwart adviser and future friend, he spent some days travelling north-west towards Huailai along the Peking-Kalgan railway. Although this line was still under construction it would eventually follow a main caravan route from Peking into Russia.

SEASON ONE 1909: To the Imperial Hunting Grounds north of Peking and across the border into Shansi

By the beginning of May, with travel permits to hand, he was on his way to Jehol and the Imperial Hunting Grounds, in the Weichang district, north of Peking. The weather was bright and the air fresh, a great improvement on the atmosphere in Peking and he was feeling in fair health. The cart had coped with the rough roads thus far, but nearer the mountains it overturned several times and even the mules struggled to maintain their footing. It took almost six days to reach Jehol and going beyond it into Weichang would only be possible by mule.

Even at this early stage, he was becoming alarmed by the impact of deforestation, 'I understand that the whole place is gradually becoming stripped of every particle of plant life… for quite one hundred miles there is hardly a tree or shrub.' However, he had already noted acers, poplars and in particular lime trees of interest. The problem was finding specimens not already reduced to stumps. His letters to Veitch and Sargent are a curious blend of diffidence and understatement. Talking of the dire roads he remarked it was just one of those little things that had to be overlooked.

The weather in mid-May continued very cold and his health was deteriorating. He was clearly unwilling to give way to personal discomfort. Commenting on two abscesses (one like an orange) on his neck, acquired he felt sure as a result of the bad water, which although boiled proved treacherous to drink, he wrote 'I have had rather a bad time.' In spite of this he would definitely complete the tour after going a further 200 miles north of Jehol to the outlying parts of Weichang. More importantly he wrote 'the people here are very good to me.' This is one of his most significant early comments; he had already established a rapport with the Chinese people that was to remain with him for the rest of his life.

Cart transport, Peking to Jehol, 1909, © and courtesy of the
Lakeland Horticultural Society

A month later and he was near Liangpa-fu, an area with rolling sandy hills that offered some attractive plants, though not in great quantity. Apparently ten years earlier the area had been well wooded and fertile but with deforestation and priority being given to rice growing, the water courses were now empty and the atmosphere very dry.

He continued to the home of a Mongol prince, who had forbidden the cutting of trees for timber, with the result that mature trees still survived. He seemed to be an enlightened ruler as two good schools had already been built for the children of the district and at least one school master had already arrived.

Although the woodland was quite sparse he saw wolf, bear, leopard and fox on the hills; shooting animals, except in self-defence, was not encouraged in the Emperor's hunting grounds and birds of any kind were very scarce. In one of his letters to Colonel Anderson he commented that 'if all the trees go the animals will soon go as well... and are now being driven out of existence for want of cover.'

After 65 days in the field he was concerned that time was passing too quickly. The hills were covered in large rocks and progress could only be made on foot. Not only had the plants to be found, field notes and photographs made, herbarium samples prepared but each plant had to be clearly marked so that it could be located once seed had set later in the year. The deep river crossings meant that time after time his specimens were soaked and the work had to be done again.

When he had time he wrote to Veitch and Sargent separately in the hope that some of the letters would get through, as even those sent to Peking did not always arrive. This did not bode well for the despatch of seeds and he wondered whether sending parcels across the Pacific might be a better option than overland via Siberia.

By the end of August 1909 he had returned to the British Legation in Peking. Many specimens and seeds had been collected and a number lost due to torrential rains and difficult river crossings. One point particularly troubled him; the loss of photographs taken on the glass plates 'no end of mine got smashed.' He advised other travellers to carry cameras that used films instead.

How to send back seeds and cuttings safely was a problem. On returning to Peking he found precious packets of seeds intended for the Arnold Arboretum still waiting despatch. He wondered if the route through Siberia might prove quicker after all. At this point Purdom found himself in a quandary. He must travel to Wutai-shan, a sacred mountain in Shansi, before the winter closed in but also leave it in time to return to Weichang to collect ripening seed there. The collecting season was proving very short.

His first set of accounts, as requested by Sargent, covering the six months from Shanghai to 1st September, were completed in meticulous detail. This included the $200 he had borrowed from Wilson; purchases of cooking utensils, water bottle, cartridges, a tent and two pairs of rough mountain boots; gifts he had made to guides and 'natives' who had helped him; wages of his 'boys' and the $1.20 spent buying stamps.

Having obtained yet another passport, he decided to set out by rail from Peking

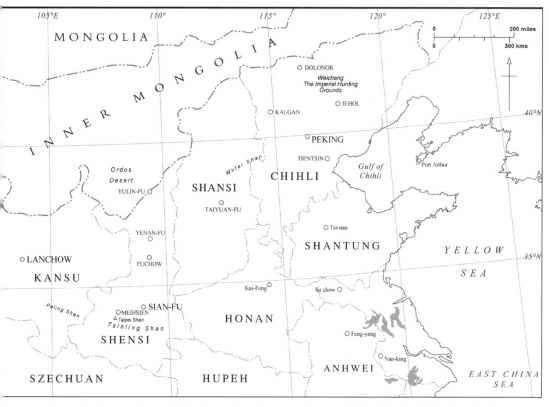

in early September via Paoting-fu, where mules could be obtained for the six day trek to Wutai-shan. Even there at 12,000 feet the area was absolutely barren, with only the temple grounds showing some interesting plants.

Rather than camp out he made his base at a temple near Wutai, where he received a friendly welcome. After three days he moved further north to an area of virgin forest where he collected seeds of *Larix* and *Picea*, despite the continuous rain, which again threatened to ruin their viability. He also made up a pack of seedlings, gathered over a wide area in the hope these living specimens would arrive safely via a steamer from Shanghai. By early October he had returned to Peking. But the seeds and plants had to be despatched before he could set out once again for Weichang. Some seeds and living plants had already arrived in London in good condition, together with specimens of *Larix*, which Veitch was already growing on at Coombe Wood.

Purdom's sister Margaret was keeping a strict eye on his finances at home and had been obliged to visit Veitch to point out that after the first payment of William's salary in June or July, she had received nothing more and it was now the end of November.

Whether Purdom expected it or not he would have to spend his first Christmas in China completely away from friends. Just before Christmas Eve he had arrived back in the now snowy south of Weichang, with the survival of his collections uppermost in his mind. As Kew and others had mentioned before he was a superb propagator and knew the importance of obtaining viable stock. His letter of 22 December 1909 asked Veitch to prepare root stocks for grafting slips of the Weichang elm, in case those he had already sent to America did not survive.

As the weather grew colder wild animals were more evident; wolf, leopard, a type of jackal, fox, deer, badger and wildcat could be seen. These did not present the same danger as the highwaymen who infested the mountain areas. Purdom's party were attacked twice; once at night and then in a separate ambush on Purdom and his 'boy' on a mountain pass. Fortunately neither attempt was successful; Purdom's main concern was for the villagers, whose grain stores were under constant threat.

His letters to Harry Veitch reveal travelling in this area had once again proved challenging. He found Dolonor a filthy place where the water was 'not fit for pigs to drink' and this again had affected his health. Although attacked by bandits he was saddened to say that the locals had had the worst of it being 'shot and robbed wholesale'; but again the villagers treated him well. Returning to Peking in January 1910 he despatched not only seedling conifers but also grafts of elms, limes and oak to Veitch.

He asked Veitch to send him a new shutter and glass plates for the camera, a waterproof ground sheet, a small axe and rather poignantly balls of string and sealing wax. It is curious to note that Veitch felt it necessary to advise Sargent that he had sent these items, without waiting for approval, as after all, they were not very expensive. As February passed preparations for the new collecting season began. His six monthly expense sheet was due and the one for 1909-10 (i.e. ending March 1910) included everything from a hammer, more balls of string, Chinese name cards, a spade and gun cartridges, to hiring boys and labourers and allowing himself the luxury of rickshaws to get about Peking. A dollar was spent on screws, nails and wire and $15.20 on medicine.

SEASON TWO 1910: Through Shansi into Shensi and the great mountains of the Tsinling and Peling ranges.

In late February Purdom's health had again proved a problem and although recovering from a heavy cold he had managed to despatch a large consignment including boxes of grafts. In April he wrote that though feeling unwell he had finally managed to arrange the journey through Shansi into Shensi and with luck would locate the 'Moutan-shan' and from there head towards Sian'fu (Xi'an) and the Tsinling Mountains.

He was optimistic that this would be a productive area since it was so little known, having only been covered by a Russian party fifteen years earlier. Again Colonel Anderson had given him as much information as he could ('secret service') on the route he was to follow; arranged the making of mule boxes; found him a copy of Rockhill's *Land of the Lamas* and above all helped him to feel at home in China.

Gate in the Great Wall, Shansi, © and courtesy of the Lakeland Horticultural Society

He knew he would have to be careful travelling down through Shansi, as troops were having difficulty maintaining order around Tai-yuan-fu due to disputes over the opium crop; several had already been killed.

After two months he arrived in Sian-fu and was pleased to meet Sir Alexander Hosie again, who was investigating the cultivation of the opium poppy. Many villages in Shensi were small and remote; the people were poor but, providing sufficient food could be stored to see them through the harsh winters, they were surprisingly content. However, opium was having an increasingly devastating effect. Some travellers mentioned the 'opium villages', where the inhabitants had lost all interest in cultivating their fields or bringing in the harvest and were slowly starving to death. Sir Alexander had been gathering reports from local authorities about their efforts to drastically reduce if not totally eliminate the opium crop. He had been assured by a local missionary that the poppy had not been seen to the south of Sian-fu.

On the way to the Tsinling Range and the sacred Taipei-shan, rising to over 12,000 feet, Purdom wrote to Hosie on 21 June that the poppy could be seen growing in patches between the grain crops and that 'three parts of the way from Wei Ho to the Chi'ing-ling [Tsinling] range of mountains was taken up with it... Nearly every man smokes opium, and, worse than that quite a large number of the womenfolk are addicted to the habit.'

The Taipei-shan was to be one of Purdom's most successful collecting locations. Here he found the *Rhododendron* named after him, a distinct rosy barked *Betula,* seven species of primula, a fine white *Potentilla* and much more. He arrived at the foot of the mountain after a week of torrential rain, where the normal streams had changed into raging torrents making the way totally impassable for the mules. A few labourers were eventually persuaded to carry his baggage and the ascent of the mountain began. It was a local tradition for the inhabitants to climb the mountain in July to offer tributes of silver, food or opium to the priests. As the weather worsened both priests and pilgrims accused him of causing the torrential downpours; it was obvious the foreigner had displeased the local gods. The lives of himself and his party were under threat.

It was a serious situation; in desperation at dusk, he sent down one of his men disguised as a pilgrim to raise help. The escape was not revealed to the priests until two days later. Although the prospect of help arriving deterred some, other leaders of the unrest continued their threats. It took the man over two days simply to reach the bottom of the mountain and then he had to make his way to the authorities in Sian-fu. He carried a message for Colonel Anderson, who once again came to the rescue by contacting the Foreign Office in Peking. Instructions were telegraphed to Sian-fu and the necessary documents were immediately issued to ensure Purdom's safety. When these arrived the attitude of the local priests changed dramatically. The very men who had threatened his life now brought food and presents to his camp.

Although now safe, he was beset by further problems. Several of his men became very sick and his interpreter nearly died on the summit. He had to get them to a hospital in Sian-fu as quickly as possible. His chief man Mafu proved indispensable.

His first intention had been to split the party leaving half to concentrate on collecting in the mountains and the others to return to Yenan-fu for the *Moutan* seeds. Now the group was so reduced this could no longer be done; so a further

William Purdom and Mafu, © and courtesy of the Lakeland Horticultural Society

six days were spent climbing Tai-pei-shan again, where they could work together. When they left the mountain at the end of September the summit was already covered in two feet of snow, but at the lower levels the autumn colours were glorious. Having described all this to Veitch he ended his letter with a laconic 'Sorry you're having it so wet in England.'

The 13 October saw him back at Sian-fu with a backlog of post from Sargent waiting for him. There was not a moment to lose; he hastened to Yenan-fu to collect the seed ripening there. Writing to Sargent at the end of the month, he apologised for being delayed through 'a little trouble with the natives' and regretted he had only managed to collect 530 *Moutan* seeds, not as much as he had expected, and just two pounds of *Pyrus sinensis*... but it was a start.

The effort to please all parties was certainly proving a problem. While he was collecting herbaceous plants for Veitch and trees for the Arnold Arboretum, and despite all the setbacks, he had managed to make the separate collections of ferns for Dr Christ and aconites for Dr Stapf, as requested by Sargent.

On his return to Peking, he was concerned to discover that post via the Siberian route had either been lost or seriously delayed. The weather remained very cold and the dust storms were particularly trying throughout January and February. He was now doing his utmost to despatch any remaining seeds almost daily. Any remaining time was spent planning the next season's journey to the province of Kansu.

It appears that despite having made all this effort Sargent was not entirely satisfied with his progress. Seemingly he expected more and, more importantly, better. Apparently Sargent was unaware or was not prepared to acknowledge that during the festive season of Christmas and New Year, there would be delays; also that the continuous rain had damaged many herbarium specimens.

What was Purdom to say? His letter of 22 January 1911 to Sargent finds him in low spirits. 'I know it is difficult for people away from the interior not to understand why things do not come to hand quicker, but regarding myself I try to do my best in matters strange to me... I am deeply sorry if I have displeased you in any way... I was so busily engaged in keeping things going.'

His account for the period until 15 February 1911 includes a strongbox for silver; the payment of bribes to anti-foreign people in the Shansi, Yellow River area; obstinate boatmen (twice); and money stolen by hostile priests, for which he asked Sargent to debit his account.

Having travelled in uncharted territory; rescued some of his party from the top of Taipei-shan; lost the services of his interpreter through sickness; encountered unfriendly natives; found the formerly satisfactory route for despatch of letters and samples via Siberia unreliable and, at the time of writing, in the throes of a 'fair dose of rheumatism', one might possibly appreciate his plea that he had done his best. However, it was inevitable that he would be compared to the great E. H. Wilson. Rather grudgingly Sargent admits that 'on the whole Purdom seems to have done better in the way of seeds than I had feared... Wilson has done magnificently.'

Perhaps their expectations of Purdom had been too high. He was less knowledgeable and experienced than Wilson and was working in a far less favourable area and on a tighter budget. He was unable to employ a large team to do any significant seed collecting on his behalf and was only thankful he could rely on a few very loyal Chinese to do some work for him.

William Purdom at Honan fu, 1911, en route for Kansu, © and courtesy of the Lakeland Horticultural Society

SEASON THREE 1911: Into Kansu and escape to Peking

Travelling through Honan, he arrived once again in Sian-fu in mid-March, despite the late snows which had made the roads difficult. His aim was to head north-west to Minchow, then cover the western part of Kansu and the Peling Mountains, finishing at the northern city of Lanchow.

William Christie, © and courtesy of the Lakeland Horticultural Society.

He was now being pressed for more information not only from Veitch and Sargent but also George Morrison (*Times* correspondent in Peking) who was particularly interested in publishing articles in *The Times* regarding the impact of deforestation.

Although Minchow at 8,000 feet looked a promising base, surrounded by fine scenery and woodlands, he found buying anything or hiring transport a 'hair turning job' as the Kansu Chinese imposed on him at every turn, especially when they saw the chance of making more money.

He was concerned about posters that were appearing in western Kansu and stirring up anti-foreign feelings. Missionaries would be particular targets. He was hoping that Mr Christie of the Christian and Missionary Alliance and expert Tibetan speaker, who had lived in Choni with his wife for some years, would be able to accompany

*Women converts to Christianity at Minchow, © and courtesy of the
Lakeland Horticultural Society*

him on part of his journey.

He found Choni and the area around the Tow River offered the best flora he had seen so far and was particularly well wooded towards the Tibetan border. The Prince in Choni, ruling over 48 Tibetan clans proved friendly. He was able to take photographs of many diverse ethnic and tribal groups including Drokwa, Tepos, Amdo border types, priests, children and Moslems.

While Purdom was enthusing about the fine display of red, yellow and blue *Meconopsis*, six species of *Primula* and yet again his favourite rosy barked *Betula*, at home Veitch was recommending a halt to the expedition at the end of the season; saying the lease on the nursery at Coombe Wood was due to expire and he had no plans to extend it. His nephew, who might have continued the nursery, had been in poor health and also agreed that it would be best if Purdom came home.

At that stage Veitch felt it best not to hint to Purdom that this was the case but asked Sargent to handle the termination of his engagement. In many ways Veitch seemed to expect Sargent to take on this unpleasant task, tempering his own suggestion with the fact that anything received from this point on would be unlikely to develop fully before the Coombe Wood nursery closed. Then by way of putting in a good word for Purdom 'if the trees and plants were not there, he could not send them.'

Poor Purdom; whilst he was receiving an encouraging note from Sargent on his arrival in Kansu, Sargent had a few days later, made the chilling comment to Veitch 'I do not think there is any necessity for his going home by way of the United States.' If Purdom had harboured any hopes that his hard work might have been rewarded with a renewal of the offer to work at the Arnold Arboretum, then he was going to be disappointed.

The last letter they seem to have received from him was sent from Minchow, dated 5 August telling of his intention to go to Monastery of Labrang, subject to permission from the priests, who had not been in favour thus far. If all went well he might be able to reach Sining-fu, north of Lanchow. What did Sargent think about this?

Although no letters came, Purdom had still been following the planned route

Watching Fenwick Owen leaving Choni, by William Purdom.
© The Royal Geographic Society

and had met big game hunters Harold F. Wallace and George Fenwick Owen in the Choni area in mid-October. He accompanied them for some days, sharing their camp and hunting expeditions. It must have been a great solace to have their companionship after being alone for so long. After one bitterly cold night and a particularly stiff trek across the hills, Wallace commented that Purdom was quite 'done up'.

In October, with still no news, Sargent displayed uncharacteristic concern about Purdom's safety, given the news that China was in an extremely unsettled state. Revolution against the Manchu dynasty and government was widespread, Shensi being a flash point and missionaries a particular target. Different factions fought each other, some murdering foreigners and other revolutionaries trying to protect them.

Mr Christie was keeping careful watch on the developing unrest and sent a note on 11 November to say the Mohammedans were rising and that the Chinese were flocking into Choni for safety. The consensus of opinion was that Wallace and Fenwick-Owen should leave Choni and the Minshan without further delay. Purdom and Mr Christie saw them off at the city gates.

A few days later Purdom managed to get through to Minchow, but he was marooned. Bands of robbers were busy plundering the area and with no responsible government it was impossible to hire mules and travel. The secret society, known as the Ko Lao Hui, (Society of the Elder Brethren), were a major problem. The society appealed to peasants, simple artisans and the common soldier. Its members were mostly illiterate, even its leaders had little education. Their aims were to kill all foreigners and government officials. Back in England Veitch was anxiously writing 'I hope Purdom will come out safely... we continue to receive seeds from him... but are still without any letter'. Despite this he simply did not seem to have grasped the seriousness of the situation and assumed the lack of letters was down to Purdom being a poor correspondent.

One letter from Purdom to sister Madge dated 3 December finally got through to England in late January 1912, possibly via Turkestan, as all roads south were cut off and post runners did not dare travel that way. He explained he was 'in a bit of a fix... western Kansu just now is very uneasy and daily risings are expected. You will know by a previous letter that I will come home via Siberia so if only I could get through it would not be long to get to England... Well I do not know how things will go before I get out of this maze but hope for the best. Yours lovingly Will, PS All quiet up to 9 December.'

A week later and Purdom was still in Minchow where the local robbers were threatening to kill him and his party. In spite of this he was still trying to pack seeds ready for despatch, if ever the opportunity arose.

In her late 80s Purdom's sister Nell recalled a little of his desperate escape from Minchow to Peking. He had employed a Mohammedan guard of three men to escort him to Sian-fu, but they had had to fight their way to safety. Attacked by bandits who shot two of their horses, Purdom greatly regretted he had been obliged to kill five Chinese and wound others and their horses to get clear.

Moslem Escort from Kansu, 1911, © and courtesy of the
Lakeland Horticultural Society

Arriving at last at Sian-fu he met Mrs and Miss Soothill (Nell called her Miss Sutille), who were about to leave the mission station and accompanied them to Peking, where he left them in the care of the Commercial Attaché Sir Alexander Hosie. Miss Soothill would later become Lady Hosie.

It was not until 21 March 1912 that he was able to send a cable announcing his safe arrival in Peking.* In a letter that followed a few days later he confirmed

---

* "A BRATHAY MAN IN CHINA, News has been received of the safe arrival at the British Legation, Peking, of Mr William Purdom…" (*Westmorland Gazette,* 30 March 1912).

Sir Alexander Hosie, William Purdom, Miss Dorothea Soothill and Mrs Soothill.
© British Library Board.

he was sending off the remaining seeds and although his contract had officially ended in February, he would try to obtain for Sargent seeds or plants of the fabled *Aesculus chinensis*. Typically he apologised for any delay but he was rather run down; there had been no shelter and very little food on the way down from Kansu.

Again the reaction of Veitch and Sargent lacked a degree of understanding. Of course their priority had been commercial gain from new and rare plants. Did anything that Veitch had sent to Boston go down with the *Titanic*, asked Sargent. If all that had arrived was the sum of Purdom's efforts then he hadn't made a great haul. Sargent had forgotten that he had chosen the location and perhaps was unlikely to admit, at this stage when he was so disappointed, that the plants simply were not there to be collected.

61

Purdom's article about the *Aesculus chinensis* was published on 9 November 1912 in *The Gardeners' Chronicle* explaining how rare the tree was and that it was regarded as sacred by the priests. According to Sir Alexander Hosie its Chinese name was *So Lo Shu* and Professor Giles believed that this related to *Sa La* in Sanskrit and so might well be the species of tree under which Buddha was born and died.

Aesculus chinensis, © and courtesy of the
Lakeland Horticultural Society

On 24 April Purdom purchased his tickets home from Peking to Harbin (three changes) and then for the international train (Trans-Siberian Railway) leaving Harbin on 9 May via Ostend and Dover for London, where he arrived on 19 May. He wrote without delay to Sargent the next day from Madge's address. Although he had only arrived at 10.15pm the previous night he described the attack sustained in Honan and, of more concern to Sargent, the loss of some boxes of material as well as his field notes and accounts.

Luckily he still had his pocket book notes from which to produce a new set of records. Conscientious to the last he pointed out that his contract had expired on 3 February 'and in view of the unfortunate situation the expedition has been placed in and the absence of novelties I do not wish the extended time taken over the trip (owing to the revolution in China) to be considered in my personal account.' He would be returning the balance of £105 to Veitch accordingly.

Veitch (now Sir Harry), asked for Sargent's advice about any payments due and Sargent surprisingly replied 'I think he ought to be treated liberally.' He was delighted to hear of the *Aesculus chinensis* plants which Purdom had managed to obtain 'we have all been trying for years to get this species into cultivation,' and 'his discovery and introduction of the wild *Moutan peony* I think is a first rate achievement.'

There also remained the fern collection Purdom had made in Shensi for Dr Christ of Basle, who although an expert in this field, was unable to take on the identification of the specimens due to ill health. These were forwarded to Carl Christensen, of the Botanical Museum, Copenhagen, who found that there were nineteen new to the province and eight new species or varieties. Sargent agreed to have the findings published and wrote to Purdom that a new variety of *Athyrium mongolicum* would be named after him. The article published in *The Botanical Gazette* in October 1913 under the heading '*Filices Purdomianae*' listed 63 ferns, most of which were collected on Tai-pei Shan in 1910.

Sargent also felt it was unfair of Veitch to compare Purdom's performance with Wilson's great successes; Wilson had travelled in an area with a far greater diversity of flora than could be found in the northern provinces. He wrote to Purdom saying how glad he was to hear of his safe return and thanking him for all he had done for the Arboretum.

Perhaps it was because of the closure of Coombe Wood and the dispersal of all its stock; his obligations to the forthcoming International Exhibition; family concerns, financial issues or some other reason, but Veitch seemed in a far less sanguine frame of mind as the expedition ended. He felt the results had been very disappointing.

Sargent on the other hand was far more positive and already considering what opportunities might lie in further foreign exploration. After all both he and Veitch were young and had many years ahead of them. He urged Veitch not to be discouraged by the worsening unrest in the UK and elsewhere. He appreciated times were bad but there would always be a future in horticulture. 'The only way to keep young and happy is to be optimistic.'

*Opposite and following pages, studies from both expeditions by William Purdom, ©
and courtesy of the Lakeland Horticultural Society. Clockwise from top left: Tibetan
men from the border region; Tibetan child in Choni;
living Buddha on right; Tibetan woman.*

*This page, clockwise from top left:
Chinese Tibetan children at Sining;
Traditional dress worn by Choni women; a
girl from the Lo-ta-ni people.*

*Opposite page, clockwise from top left: Kansu
Moslems; Tatung Tibetans; Business Lama at
Chebson Abbey; Tibetan woman.*

6
Difficult Years 1912-13

On his return to London in late May Purdom's priority had been to write up the information from his pocket book notes; complete his accounts for Veitch and Sargent and forward any remaining photographs and seeds.

In early June he finally had the chance to spend a fortnight at home with his parents. He must have had such mixed feelings: relief at surviving; disappointment that it could all have gone so much better; making every effort to put on a brave face and worrying about the future.

Did his fiancée wait for him? According to a close neighbour of Brathay Lodge, he had certainly sent back gifts for her. But three years would have been a long time to wait, especially during those long months when they feared he was dead. If she had not and he still cared for her, then the sense of defeat and disillusion would have been all the greater.

Purdom was prone to bouts of low spirits. He had been unlucky in the area chosen, the political unrest and now the pending closure of the Veitch Nurseries. The feeling that he was a failure, not necessarily because of his own shortcomings but because of lack of support from others, went deep and was to be a recurring theme.

Then there was China. He believed there was important work to be done in forestry if the authorities would only agree to it. Contrary to all expectations, he had learned Chinese quickly and was able to speak it using the idioms of muleteer swearing and the laughing talk of the Chinese innkeepers. China was no longer a foreign place to him; despite all the difficulties he felt at home there and ached to return.

The arrival of Frank Meyer in England in November gives an interesting insight into Purdom's state of mind. Born in Amsterdam in 1875, Meyer was undoubtedly an energetic, dedicated and prolific collector. For a number of years he had travelled widely in Mexico, California and Cuba. He was returning to China to collect plants of commercial interest for David Fairchild of the United States

Department of Agriculture. His target was Shensi and Kansu. Both Sargent and Wilson recommended he visit Purdom who would be able to provide invaluable information about these areas.

Despite his many botanical skills Meyer seemed to lack one essential gift, that of tact. He could be stubborn, obtuse and completely dismissive of the work of others. Some found it difficult to establish a rapport with him; even the genial Wilson considered him inattentive and lacking any sense of humour. Five years previously Meyer had met Wilson in Shanghai for a briefing; after which he concluded that the advice he had received about herbarium specimens, keeping detailed field notes and taking photographs was more or less a waste of his valuable time. Fairchild tolerated his abruptness and genuinely enjoyed his company.

Meyer had already visited Veitch's Coombe Wood Nursery in April 1912 and considered the little Purdom had collected was very common. He blamed Sargent for thinking that northern China would prove a gold mine for new plants. Nor was he particularly impressed with the evergreen viburnums collected by Wilson, which he found far from handsome and, even worse, covered in soot. He did concede that the Coombe Wood nurseries were really wonderful.

He also visited the great Augustine Henry in Cambridge but commented he was not satisfied with their meeting as Henry had inexplicably been unable to find any notes on the plants he collected. He also dismissed Kingdon-Ward as being rather non-communicative.

He had decided it was essential to meet Purdom before he left for China, but when he arrived in London in November he discovered that Purdom was determined to keep a low profile. Veitch, Sargent and Wilson could not or would not give him any idea as to where Purdom might be found but he was not going to give up that easily. He finally tracked down Purdom's sister Margaret, who said her brother was in the country and she would forward a letter on his behalf.

When Purdom replied he said he couldn't meet him and unfortunately failed to provide a forwarding address. After further persuasion, he reluctantly agreed to a meeting in Ambleside; a seven hour journey by train from London to Windermere. Meyer felt he had taken a great deal of trouble to meet Purdom, but was obliged to do so, since he was one of the few Europeans who had travelled widely in Shensi and Kansu. The meeting was brief with Purdom giving as an excuse pre-existing arrangements to visit relatives. Was this true or simply a desire to avoid any lengthy contact with Meyer? Perhaps he found Meyer's style of approach intrusive.

Reporting back to Fairchild, Meyer felt there was little he could say about Purdom, who had clearly travelled to the wrong place, at the wrong time and no-one seemed interested in what he had collected anyway. Meyer genuinely pitied him and likened him to a general who had lost a battle. Despite the little information Purdom was willing to provide, it was obvious he did not wish to discuss his time in China in greater detail.

Meyer certainly felt there was more to tell and added a postscript that had he been able to get him into the more convivial atmosphere of a local inn, Purdom might have revealed all that was on his mind. As it was Purdom had proved uncommunicative and gave information grudgingly. Whether Meyer took this personally is open to question, but when their paths crossed again, he did not hesitate to disparage Purdom in his letters to America.

In December 1912, with the help of his local friend and mentor Dr Hough of White Craggs, Purdom entertained local groups with magic lantern shows of his Chinese adventures. At one given to the Band of Hope and held in the schoolroom at Skelwith Bridge, he mentioned his former connection with the school. That Christmas, Dr Hough gave Purdom's mother an album of his Chinese photographs

By July 1913 he was back in London, writing from Margaret's address to Morrison in Peking, saying he found life in England rather flat after all his adventures in China. The damage caused by the deforestation weighed heavily on his mind. He had therefore enclosed an album of photographs relating to the forestry question and a detailed report on the training of forestry officers and a paper headed *The Afforestation Question of China*.

Given the unrest in China in the past two years, he was finding it difficult to contact any Chinese authorities who might be interested in his suggestions and wondered if Morrison might help. He outlined his concerns and put forward possible solutions. He felt this was something he could achieve not only for the good of China but for reputation of Britain as well.

Purdom had clearly grasped the implications on climate and soil erosion that the loss of these great forests entailed, particularly when China seemed deficient in other sustainable fuel resources. The wholesale chopping down of trees, which were then left to rot, was inexplicable. The rains caused soil and sand to run down into the valleys, widening river beds, destroying roads and leaving only the less favourable hill slopes on which to grow crops.

He also raised the problem of the encroachment of the desert sands along and

William Purdom, aged 33, © and courtesy of the
Lakeland Horticultural Society

around the Great Wall in north Shensi and which also affected the Peking Plain. The planting of soil binding plants and trees which would provide shelter from the prevailing high winds each spring, was essential. He then briefly outlined how such work might begin with the setting up of a Forestry School near Peking, where students could be trained in theoretical and practical forestry from the sowing of seeds to tree, forest and staff management.

In the pre-war years Morrison had shown a genuine interest in afforestation and agreed that there was nothing that China needed more than a Forestry Department but that the country was so unsettled that little could be done at the present time. He did, however, promise to keep Purdom's address and assured him that he would help him, if ever the opportunity arose. It might appear a somewhat dismissive reply, but an honest one.

If Purdom made any attempt to obtain employment earlier in the year then nothing came of it. He now had to make serious efforts to find a position. He had, in fact, applied for a position as superintendent of parks in Northampton. Concerned that he might be asked what he had been doing during the preceding months he explained in his application that he had been helping develop the layout of Dr Hough's garden at White Craggs. Landscape architect and garden designer Thomas Mawson was also involved in the project.

He gave Hough as a contact and told him he had received good references from Sir Harry Veitch and the curator at Kew. He hoped he stood a good chance but wondered if they might already have someone else in mind. It might simply be a coincidence but his younger brother Harry, who had also trained as a gardener, eventually became a park superintendent and lived in the Northampton area for many years. On 4 October 1913 his article on plant-collecting in China was published in *The Gardeners' Chronicle*.

Purdom's love of China and wish to return was amply expressed in this article. The photograph he chose to illustrate it, also has something of Cumbria about it. He described his 1911 season in Kansu and the borderlands of Tibet mentioning the area around Choni with particular affection. He wrote of the many opportunities to meet local people and how impressed he was by 'the haunting charm of the mountain land' and then later 'The Italian proverb says "See Naples and die"; but a traveller arriving at this spot wishes not to die, but to live forever'.

He explained that the collecting season had proved short, lasting only through June, July and August and that the climate was bracing. Where shelter from trees and shrubs was lacking the countryside was open to the mercy of piercing winds.

Tibetan village near Chapa monastery: 'The Gardeners' Chronicle', October 1913.

He advised any foreigners visiting the area to establish good relations with the tribal or clan chiefs and earn their trust, otherwise travelling in these remote areas could be difficult if not impossible.

Despite his anxieties and his sense of failure 1913 ended on a brighter note for Purdom. He was sponsored by his friend Colonel Abbot Anderson FRGS in late December to become a member of the Royal Geographic Society and was duly elected in January 1914.

There was also the chance of returning to China with Reginald Farrer on a plant collecting expedition.

7

Farrer's Plan

A keen and knowledgeable enthusiast of alpine flowers Farrer was interested in organising his own plant collecting expedition to China. On Wednesday 16 April 1913 a Primula Conference had been held by the Royal Horticultural Society in London, which he attended as a guest speaker. There he saw *Primula purdomii*, which had been given a First Class Certificate and had been inspired by it.

Professor Bayley Balfour of the Royal Botanic Garden Edinburgh had advised Farrer that his plant collecting plans were somewhat unrealistic. There was no point in going to Yunnan or the Mekong-Salween-Yangste divide, as Farrer suggested. George Forrest was already in his second season in Yunnan and employing some 100 collectors; whilst Frank Kingdon Ward had started further north towards the Burmese border and settled there well. Besides which Farrer could not hope to be successful in just a single season. At least two years would be needed. Kansu with its mountains would surely be productive and Purdom must be

Reginald Farrer, courtesy of the Royal Botanic Garden, Edinburgh, Farrer Archive.

his mentor regarding travelling in the area: 'Purdom is the man... if you can get him.'

During the summer of 1913 Farrer contacted Dr Hough and asked him to arrange a meeting with Purdom. This was done and the three of them spent an afternoon at Kew together. Hough said that they had planned the expedition to north-west China by the time they returned to London. Whether matters progressed quite that smoothly is open to question.

Farrer would be responsible for the entire project, including the funding. This would not prove easy. He approached Colonel Prain of Kew asking if the Government would give him £2,000 sponsorship. Prain could not countenance this. If granted it would create a precedent for any aspiring amateur in the future. Balfour had seen a copy of Prain's letter and had already made it clear to Farrer that requests for grants from the Treasury or state gardens, for a private expedition, would be bound to fail. Despite his undoubted knowledge Farrer was regarded as an amateur by the horticultural establishment.

The result was that the expedition was greatly underfinanced. Some funding came from A. K. Bulley of Ness, Lionel de Rothschild, members of the Farrer family, Edinburgh Botanic Garden, Frederick C. Stern, George Fenwick-Owen (whom Purdom had met in China) and the Woodward family of Arley Castle. In addition some of Purdom's neighbours in Westmorland also made a contribution. These included Dr Hough of White Craggs, Mr William Groves of Holehird near Windermere (now the site of the Lakeland Horticultural Society Gardens), Mrs Anne Marshall of Skelwith Fold near Ambleside and Miss Ripley. Each would receive a proportion of the seeds collected.

In September Purdom wrote in reply to a letter from Farrer saying that his interest in a further trip to western China had been reawakened. He believed that the south west corner of Kansu, most particularly the unexplored area of the southern slopes of the Minshan Range rising to 15-17,000 feet, would be of particular interest. He enclosed maps showing where he had found novelties.

He would be delighted to accompany Farrer and give him as much information as he could. He had only one concern and trusted Farrer would keep it confidential. He had been in touch with various people in China regarding his afforestation project. Although it was unlikely that any opportunity would arise in the short term, he could only make a firm commitment for twelve months. He would be happy to go to Peking a month before Farrer arrived, to arrange the hiring of mules, a small staff and generally make all the necessary preparations.

Perhaps Farrer might also like to use his watertight mule boxes?

Whether Purdom was overcome by Farrer's enthusiasm (they were both just 33 and drawn to China); genuinely felt there was nothing left to keep him at home; that there might be the prospect of doing something really worthwhile or that this was a chance for fame and perhaps fortune, he agreed to travel with Farrer, virtually as a servant and with no pay. Perhaps the last point was not clear until it was too late.

Purdom could have had no idea what he was taking on. He was to learn quickly. It was not long before he found himself apologising to the Westmorland contributors because Farrer had not made the financial arrangements clear. In the first year each would contribute £25 with a further £25 in the following year. Although Farrer's gardener Redman would handle the bulk of the seed distribution, each subscriber had the right to divide their share as they wished. He would write separately to Farrer asking him to provide a clearer financial statement.

Farrer was a character. Not easy and not forgiving, but generous to a fault to those he cared about. On the other hand he could be a terrible snob; often

Ingleborough Hall, author's photograph with kind permission of Ingleborough Hall Outdoor Education Centre.

convinced of his own superiority; patronising and able to exasperate close friends and relatives with extraordinary ease.

The Farrer family was wealthy and cultivated. During the first half of the nineteenth century they made substantial changes to the house and area surrounding Ingleborough Hall (formerly a shooting lodge). It appears the family valued their privacy above all things and took a rather strange way to ensure it To avoid being overlooked by people passing along a nearby lane, alterations were made which allowed the Farrers to access their gardens without being seen. Staff had to use a tunnel some 80m long to arrive at their working quarters at the back of the Hall. In later years this arrangement may well have affected Farrer's sense of isolation from the lower orders and possibly reinforced his sense of superiority.

Farrer suffered greatly as a child, being born with a hare lip and cleft palate. Numerous operations and ill health meant he spent his early years close to his mother. He was no doubt spoiled. Their mutual affection remained throughout their lives. It was not until his mid-teens that he was able to speak clearly enough to be understood by others. He was able to roam the nearby fells and develop his own rock garden and nursery at Ingleborough without any major financial concerns.

There had been a hope that Farrer would find his future in the Church. His mother, a strikingly handsome woman according to Osbert Sitwell, Farrer's second cousin, was deeply devoted and committed to good works, charitable activities, family prayer and missionary meetings. Sundays could be oppressive and the influence of the 'aunts' suffocating. When Farrer returned home from a tour in Asia as a Buddhist '...his mere presence in the house struck a chill to the bones of the faithful.'

Osbert had some revealing comments to make. He did not come to know Farrer until the later years of the First World War, although he had heard much about him through family connections. His sister Edith Sitwell, who often stayed with Mr and Mrs Farrer in Yorkshire, knew Farrer well and was fond of him – unlike some others she appreciated his wit. Osbert also saw a different side to Farrer to that mentioned in his letters and books. Although Farrer often claimed to be most a ease in the solitude of the mountains, yet he was sociable and enjoyed stimulating company.

To compensate for his rather strange appearance (short, low browed and with an abundant moustache to hide his hare lip), he adopted an affected manner and according to Osbert, held forth in a voice that '...sounded like one of those early gramophones fitted with a tin trumpet.' He particularly disliked hypocrisy and pretentiousness in others and did not hesitate to challenge it whenever the mood took him.

When at Baliol, Oxford, he was captivated by fellow student Aubrey Herbert, half-brother of Lord Carnarvon the Egyptologist, and wrote to him endlessly. Herbert, a future Tory MP and fearless traveller throughout the Ottoman Empire was charming and yet careless of others' feelings. He invited Farrer to his home at Picton in Somerset and asked him to join visits to Japan and Italy. He then neglected to answer Farrer's outpourings in either a prompt or kindly fashion, leaving Farrer bereft and bewildered.

Farrer simply ached to be accepted into that special coterie, which included Raymond Asquith and T. E. Lawrence. Somehow he never seemed to strike quite the right note. This was especially true when it came to Herbert's wife Mary, who described him as 'a malevolent gnome, with a wish to be fascinating but an ill-restrained bitterness of tongue.'

During his brief life, Farrer's literary output was extraordinary. He published fifteen books (horticultural and fiction), produced copious and detailed articles for the horticultural press and wrote constantly to friends and relations. One wonders how he found time to collect plants, let alone produce exquisite watercolour studies of flowers in situ. Such was the character of the man Purdom agreed to accompany in China. Before leaving he gave a solemn promise to Farrer's mother to take care of her beloved son, though at times he would come to regret it.

8
The Kansu Expedition 1914-15

The Eaves of the World and *The Rainbow Bridge* give Farrer's version of the Kansu expedition. Ranging in style from a *Boys' Own* adventure to the deepest of purple prose, they may baffle, irritate or delight the reader in equal measure. Perseverance will reveal something of his character and his genuine love of mountains and alpine plants. However, his version of some events was not always reliable.

Farrer points out that Purdom had agreed to travel with no more reward than his expenses and the pleasure of Farrer's company. With their different social standing and experience would they be able to get on?

Much has been made about the difference in character between the ebullient Farrer and reticent Purdom but they shared many qualities too. They were undoubtedly courageous; united by a shared love of plants; unlikely to suffer fools gladly and neither would have taken kindly to a put down real or imagined. Both had a sense of the ridiculous and a much needed sense of humour. As the expedition progressed Farrer would come to view Purdom not just as a useful, unpaid servant but as someone who had earned his increasing respect and genuine friendship.

There has been some speculation as to the nature of their relationship. Farrer's letters to Aubrey Herbert in particular seem emotionally charged; but it was a style often used by public school boys and the Oxford set. Different times and different ways of expressing that contact apply. Farrer did explore the attraction between men and women in his 1907 book *The Sundered Streams* where the heroine is reincarnated as a young man to the confusion of her former (eternal) lover.

Purdom had promised Farrer's mother that he would ensure his safety and well-being. It is abundantly clear that when Purdom made a promise he kept it. His solicitous care of Farrer should be taken simply as that – a duty and a promise.

Opposite Farrer's seating plan and timetable for the Trans-Siberian journey,
courtesy of the Royal Botanic Garden, Edinburgh, Farrer Archive.

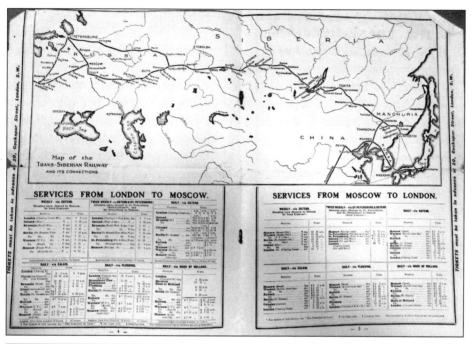

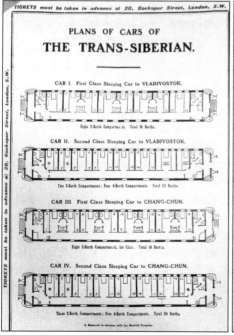

Mrs Joan Farrer explained that Purdom was a strong character and had the wisdom to break away from camp from time to time; either to collect plants or recover from the suffocating presence of Farrer. The temperaments of both men needed isolation on occasion.

Purdom may have been the quieter of the two but was undoubtedly a great communicator and skilled organiser in his own right. He travelled to Peking on the Trans-Siberian railway (lower class) two months ahead of Farrer, who followed in superior class, to establish the groundwork of engaging mule teams, Chinese bearers and stores. His knowledge of the Chinese language made him indispensable. Farrer commented that Purdom was 'an especially admirable conductor and companion who gets on famously with the Chinese... He is on the best of terms with minor officials of the Legation, so that a hundred necessary and otherwise expensive little jobs, are put through immediately for love instead of money.'

Arriving in Peking in late January 1914, Purdom lost no time in contacting Morrison and suggesting an introduction as soon as Farrer arrived. In the meantime he was lucky to re-establish contact with Mafu who with his brother Go-go would prove the mainstay of the team.

As time passed a cook, recommended by Mafu, totally failed to impress 'neither could he cook, nor did he make the slightest effort to acquire that useful art'; even preparing a scrambled egg seemed beyond him. Farrer often complained that he would languish for days on just honey, toast and tea, which suggests he couldn't scramble an egg either. Although he was a Buddhist Farrer did not seem to have become a complete vegetarian.

During the early months of the expedition, Mrs Farrer sent, via E. Lazenby & Son Ltd or the Army and Navy Co-operative Stores in London, parcels of delicacies to her beloved son. On 16 April 1914, Lazenby's advised her 'brigand difficulties have arisen in Sian Fu, and trouble may be experienced in the transmission of parcels by the trans-Siberian Route... we are advised to send your parcels to The British Embassy at Pekin.'

The fact that they received these parcels at all (some despatched direct to Sian Fu or Tsin Chow) must be down to his mother's determination and the resilience of the often maligned Chinese postal service and its carriers.

Peking had changed since Purdom left in 1912. Yuan Shih-k'ai, after a brief and unsuccessful insurrection in the south, known as the Second Revolution, advised the ex-Emperor Pu Yi, that he had been elected President. He was going to 'lead the people to good government and order'. According to Pu Yi there was hope amongst the palace officials that 1914 might be the year of his restoration; this is how he remembered the situation in later life. He was barely eight years old at the time and living in a quasi-fantasy world where the trappings of Emperor were maintained but his power and that of the palace administrators was effectively nil.

The political situation was unstable to an alarming degree. There were times when Yuan Shih-k'ai seemed to lean towards some kind of restoration of the Manchu dynasty. At others, when the Republic's Inspectorate enquired about these rumours, he resolutely declared 'Rumours about a restoration are severely prohibited' following this up with an enigmatic request that the investigation should not be too thorough. Yuan would continue to vacillate, eventually becoming Emperor himself and suggesting Pu Yi should marry one of his daughters. He

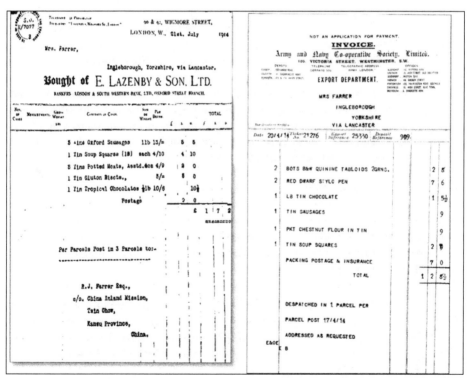

Sausages, soup squares and supplies for the soda siphons were particular favourites, courtesy of Mrs Joan Farrer.

died in June 1916 after 83 days on the throne.

It would be unfair to suggest that Farrer simply did what he wanted to do and left all the routine drudgery to others. On the other hand, he made it quite clear that he was not to be involved in everyday routine. In moving from place to place, Purdom would go ahead, find suitable lodgings and prepare everything for Farrer's arrival. The rooms in the inns were chosen with care; if a long stay was envisaged walls might be papered; Farrer's special camp bed either raised onto a 'kang',* if it were cold, or onto some other platform well away from the ravages of fleas and bedbugs. Purdom was at times obliged to sleep on saddles or mule packs on the inn floors.

Throughout the journey Farrer continually prepared articles for *The Garden Chronicle;* the *Royal Horticultural Society Journal;* worked on proofs for his two volume book *The English Rock Garden*; sent letters home and amassed notes for the three subsequent books on the expedition; and found time to take photographs, paint watercolour studies, collect plants, make the essential field notes and organise herbarium specimens.

Purdom was proving a gifted photographer. The plants were either photographed in situ or carefully lifted and taken under cover. In addition he was greatly in demand to take the portraits of local dignitaries encountered en route. He used either 3¼ inch glass plates or occasionally a film camera; though the latter seems to have been used mainly by Farrer. Any failed glass plates were often used to repair windows in their lodgings, especially Farrer's room.

The boys also developed invaluable skills in drying and mounting the herbarium specimens, handling the plants with remarkable delicacy. Farrer was convinced of the benefits of involving them in this work which he believed encouraged their involvement in the expedition; they were more likely to take care of specimens they had prepared themselves.

As they set out from Peking on 5 March 1914, news of increased predations by the White Wolf and his army gave cause for concern. After the fall of the Manchu dynasty, unrest had prevailed over a large part of China. Much of the aggression was aimed at Yuan Shih-k'ai, who had supported the Empress Dowager and then assumed control of the government. None were truly safe; missionaries and richer local communities were the main targets. Some 50 cities in central China had already been attacked and virtually destroyed in 1913.

The White Wolf's army was made up of revolutionaries, deserters, bandits,

---

* A 'kang' is a heated raised platform of bricks or fired clay.

disbanded soldiers and disaffected peasantry. It was claimed that the White Wolf was an able leader, who gained the support of the poor by his attacks on corrupt local governors; raids on food stores were apparently redistributed to the needy. The army seemed to be split between genuine freedom fighters and a lawless rabble, which needed little excuse to rob and kill.

The army was often out of control. Old scores were settled; Muslims in particular were targeted and massacred, as were many Chinese who did not dare stand against the army for fear of reprisals; whether they remained silent or not, rape, looting and brutal killings became the norm. It was not until well into 1914 that Yuan Shih-k'ai mobilised a force against them. By then it was too late and the White Wolf could not be found. The army had left a trail of destruction through

The worst road in the Empire at Mien Chi Hsien, © and courtesy of the Lakeland Horticultural Society

Shensi and Shansi and soon it would be the turn of Kansu.

The first stage of their journey was by train with all their horses and baggage to Mien-Chi Hsien. It was a tiresome stage as the railway was badly organised. This was a minor problem when it became clear the road ahead was considered to be one of the worst in the Empire. Despite ongoing rumours, there was no sign of the White Wolves, but they kept their guns well-oiled and their powder dry. Farrer, though feeling the cold, was in good health.

After ten difficult days they arrived in Sian, which had stood firm against the White Wolf. Farrer did not like Sian, he called it a place of dust and mud, smells and death; surrounded by the bones of dead inhabitants, dating back over 4,000 years. He felt it had little to offer and could not possibly offer any attraction for sightseers for a very long time; it would be more than 60 years before its fame was assured with the discovery of the Terracotta Army.

Several weeks passed before they could leave. Purdom had been feeling unwell during the journey to Sian. At first it seemed to be just a cold, brought on by being chilled and soaked in the inclement weather. However, it was not long before he was taken to hospital, covered in a rash that made his skin tender. Dr Young was concerned and would have liked to move him to a more comfortable location. Farrer was not at all happy about this suggestion. He was impatient at the delays and unsympathetic towards Purdom's 'so called illness', acting as if it were a joke. Purdom was almost in despair, remarking on Farrer's self-absorption and general uselessness. It took him a long time to get ready in the morning, arranging and pomading a curl on his forehead and then waxing his moustaches. Perhaps Farrer deserved a little sympathy – he was in a totally alien environment; could not understand the language and so had no idea whether his demands were being answered or ignored. He had yet to discover how to earn the respect of the Chinese. Spending an inordinate time in front of a mirror was not the way.

Completely adrift without Purdom's steadying support, he annoyed everyone about him, European and Chinese alike. He demanded immediate and constant attention and complained about the food but was more than happy to eat everything put before him. A week later, towards the end of March, Purdom was feeling a little better but Farrer was anything but congenial company. Becoming ill himself, he berated the doctors and had nothing good to say to anyone around him. The Chinese had noticed and commented on this; causing others to lose face was an unwise thing to do.

Leaving Sian was still proving difficult. The authorities felt unable to let them go while there was any threat from the White Wolves. Although they had managed to hire mules, these had to be hidden until the Chinese Foreign Office reluctantly agreed to their departure. They were fortunate – other Europeans faced much longer delays since the Chinese authorities feared reprisals from the West should any of them be harmed outside the city.

Caravan on way to Kansu, © and courtesy of the Lakeland Horticultural Society

As they crossed the flat plains, Farrer allowed himself the luxury of a sedan chair – with four bearers – in which he could keep warm, doze a little, have a snack or read a book (preferably Jane Austen). Purdom rode with the mules, boys and the two soldiers, provided as an escort. The escorts may not have looked imposing but they were a symbol of authority. The weather continued unsettled and they fought against biting winds and snow, which although it melted quickly at the lower levels, made the tracks slippery and treacherous; all struggled to keep on their feet.

Their arrival at inns attracted curious and not always friendly crowds. While Farrer assumed a dignified and haughty air to illustrate his importance, Purdom would take practical measures to gain their trust, often dealing with the various ailments of their hosts. Early in April, they left the plains of Shensi and entered Kansu. Farrer could at last see mountains in the distance and the alpine scenery so precious to him. Having changed the mules from Sian with a new team and sedan chair, they set off again. Farrer called 16 April an important date in botanical history as it marked the first discovery of *Viburnum fragrans* growing in the wild. A few days later he described a Tree Peony (*Moutan*) in flower; white with 'featherings of deepest maroon', sounding very like a form of *Paeonia rockii*.

As they entered Kiai-jo the situation became increasingly unsettled; it had almost the atmosphere of a lawless Wild West frontier town. Streets were crowded, a fight had broken out and their reception was far from friendly. This was the time a pigtail might 'easily involve the lack or continued possession of the head' that wore it. No inn was available for them and uproar prevailed but here again Purdom's diplomacy and Chinese skills saved the day. It was not long before accommodation was found and smiling courtesies ensued.

Heading south towards Wen Hsien they avoided meeting the army of the White Wolf, but again no preparations had been made for their arrival. Riding ahead Purdom was obliged to solve the problem by commandeering an empty house. For the present they were both feeling fit and well and Farrer was behaving normally. In the articles he sent to *The Gardeners' Chronicle* he was careful not to give the names of the places they visited and devised his own translations into German, French or used English transliterations – whatever took his fancy. The reason for this was that plant collectors were very wary of revealing their precise location, until the seeds or plants they discovered had been officially identified and attributed.

Considerable anxiety arose when their plan to cross into Tibet became known. The mountainous border area into Tibet had a terrible reputation and had always been unsafe for strangers. They knew they would not be welcome, but still continued, arriving there during the first week of May. Inadvertently Farrer had already managed to cross a sacred path and the local Prior at Chago made his dissatisfaction at their arrival quite clear. Then appearing to relent, when he discovered Farrer was a Buddhist, gave them the impression that they were now welcome. He was at the same time, according to Farrer, arranging for them to be murdered while they slept.

They realised that they could not remain safely in Tibet and reluctantly left the promising mountains and returned with relief to the more friendly Chinese side of the border. Mafu had been sent to obtain the necessary permissions from the Mandarins in Siku to make Satani their base for the summer. On his return they learned that Kansu had been invaded by the White Wolf and that Siku itself might

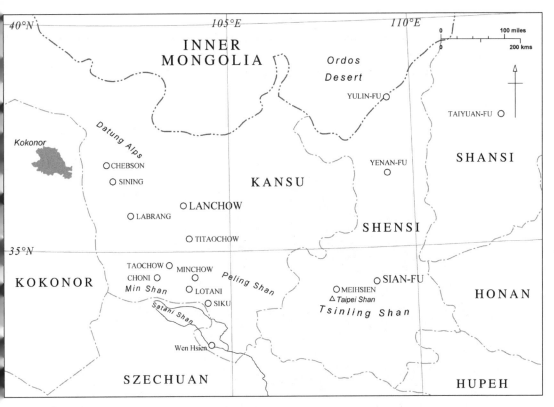

be a target.

The weather during the middle two weeks in May continued unsettled with cloudless skies turning to rain or sleet as evening approached. Farrer waxed lyrical about the spring flowers, particularly the pink blossoms of peonies, flowering currants, roses and the woods of red birch rising to meet the dark conifer forests above. This was going to be a perfect site for their summer exploration.

However, the Wolves had other ideas. The authorities in Siku were in a quandary. It seemed likely that the whole area was about to fall. Should the foreigners be sheltered in Siku or allowed to remain in the remote valleys and so avoid being found? Either way if anything happened to them the Mandarins would be held responsible. Accurate information was non-existent and rumours were rife; Siku was a blood bath; the storms (caused by their presence in the countryside) of the past few days had destroyed the annual corn crop; all were against them.

89

The kind local people they had met in Satani could not possibly protect them from the anger of priests, Tibetans, Wolves and whoever else might decide to take against them. They expected an imminent attack. Their party of six plus a small boy, who had acted as a guide took up position. Farrer's own words paint a vivid picture:

The defence of Siku: manning the western gate, © and courtesy of the
Lakeland Horticultural Society

...with teeth chattering like castanets, what with the cold and the excitement... our armoury comprised that shotgun of erratic tendencies, a rifle, three revolvers, and a very elegant sword-stick that now got firmly stuck in its socket... We disposed our men... and constructed a laager all along the veranda-front of the big black boxes that contained our silver and our specimens... And thus, in a fine martial glow, we awaited the coming of the enemy and of the grey dawn.

The attack did not come but they had to get away. Their presence was a danger to their friends. Working down through the valleys they did not find the devastation they expected. Protected by its walls Siku was not a ruin, although none had dared leave it for several weeks; for whatever reason the Wolves had passed it by on their way north. There was now time to relax and be welcome. But the feeling of security did not last long, for news came of hostile forces approaching from Tibet.

The gates were again closed; the walls manned and watch fires lit. The night passed without incident but a scouting party of Tibetans had been seen in the morning. Farrer and Purdom found themselves besieged on two fronts; the Tibetans and Wolves on the outside and the Mandarins (refusing them permission to leave) on the inside. It was now the end of May and they were losing precious time.

A few days later a force of troops from Szechuan arrived to raise the siege. The situation was far from clear with conflicting rumours of where the Wolves were and who was supporting them – Tibetans, local Mohammedans or belligerent monks from Chago. The troops began a series of punitive raids, which only added to the unrest and wounded soldiers returned to Siku. Although for the most part their wounds were not severe, Farrer, Purdom and their precious medicine chest were in great demand.

It was almost a month before it was considered safe enough for them to leave, and head north-west. Farrer lapsed into his most purple prose when describing the plants and the places they visited. Even the most dedicated reader might be reduced to hysteria when confronted by 'Proud Margaret' and 'Woolyhair the Dwarf', echoes coming from the Schlucht, and an ascent 'finding for this nameless eminence of the great Min S'an Ridge only the unpatriotic designation of the Roterdspitze, after that russet neck which ties the Schlern at right angles to the Rosengarten chain.'

The mountain he called Thundercrown certainly lived up to its name, as deafening thunder accompanied by gales, torrential rain and sleet lashed their camp. Farrer bewailed the fact that he was in the smaller tent and felt 'as if I were

*Camp near the foothills of Min Shan, 1914, © and courtesy of the
Lakeland Horticultural Society*

in an angry green balloon… [which] threatened every moment to depart into space,
till at last I bolted for safety into the big tent,' where he discovered conditions
were even worse.

Returning again to Siku, they received a letter from Mr Christie confirming it
was now safe to travel to Minchow. There was still considerable difficulty in
getting letters through, but as soon as the postal service was open again, precious
seeds were despatched to Redman, at the Craven Nursery for distribution. The
only exception was Mr Fenwick-Owen's share, which he had asked to be sent
direct. Farrer was apparently reluctant to give away too many of the good things
to his sponsors, which exasperated Purdom. After receiving Christie's reassuring
letter, they discovered that the White Wolves had murdered 400 in Minchow and
10,000 in Taochow (the figures for these incidents are also reported as 1,000 and
7,000 respectively). Women and girls had been abused and killed in such a horrific
fashion that Purdom was sickened by the barbarism.

Mr Christie, his family and fellow missionaries, had had an equally dangerous
time, since the mission stations were prime targets. The Wolves had attacked the
Minchow Mission and demanded not only money and all valuables, but also the

women. Knowing that female missionaries must be hiding somewhere, they threatened Christie's life. It was only through the self-sacrifice of a Chinese convert, who was carried off by the Wolves, that the missionary families were finally able to escape.

Taking advantage of the safety offered by the presence of an official from the Viceroy of Kansu, the expedition followed him to Choni and a meeting with Mr Christie. Farrer's attitude towards the mission stations and their staff was ambivalent. He was more than happy to stay, since he was usually given the best rooms and was well fed. However, this did not prevent him from upsetting people, much to Purdom's embarrassment and shame. His behaviour only improved when he needed help.

Ruins of Taochow, photograph by William Purdom, © The Royal Geographic Society.

Despite his opinion of missionaries in general, Farrer found Mr Christie 'apart from the eccentricities of his religious views, about which nobody need trouble' an admirable man. The long years spent in the Tibetan borderlands had given Mr Christie a rare knowledge of the language, people, customs and local politics. Through his good relations with the Prince of Choni, he was permitted to guide Farrer through the massive abbey complex; possibly one of the largest in the world. With Mr Christie as interpreter the highlight of his visit was an audience with the Living Buddha of Nalang, the most sacred person in the abbey.

Towards the end of July they left for the foothills of the Min Shan and the Stone Mountains. River crossings proved a challenge as horses and mules had to swim, be loaded onto rope-ferries or use the cantilever bridges. Faced with a bridge of dubious stability, Farrer typically refused to follow Purdom's example and dismount; he urged his horse forward. The horse having none of this, sidled towards the edge where the railings had broken, and fell over the side into the river below. Farrer made light of the adventure afterwards, but when he and the horse were 'no longer one but two' was convinced this really was his end. He was 'consumed only with rage over so ignominious a conclusion... The least he [Purdom] could have done... was to jump in and perish also.'

Tibetan bridge near Choni, © and courtesy of the Lakeland Horticultural Society

Tracks were limited or non-existent; ascents steep with loose rocks, boulders and scree obstructing the way. Visibility was often lost as cloud descended. Even though this was barely the end of July, the unpredictability of the weather with its bitter winds at high altitudes and persistent rain slowed their progress significantly. During fine spells they were obliged to split up and collect separately; either on different sides of a valley or at different levels. Even when the weather did improve and the Stone Mountains could be seen clearly all day, they were still out of reach, many miles away.

All too soon it was time to turn back. To make the most of the seed harvest they decided that Purdom would remain in Choni while Farrer headed for Siku. As they again prepared to go their separate ways, a local missionary arrived with a telegram saying that France and Germany were at war. Britain's position was unknown.

Farrer was about to realise how much he had taken Purdom's reassuring presence for granted. He now felt alone with only the indispensable Mafu, two other staff, three soldiers and four donkey men to take care of him; the point being

Sacred yak, © and courtesy of the Lakeland Horticultural Society

they could not speak English and his command of Chinese was minimal. Despite the occasional glorious day, rain fell in deluges; rivers flooded and bridges were washed away. Farrer's relief in arriving in Siku in a heatwave was palpable. However, he now had time was able to reflect on the costs – financial and physical – that plant collecting entailed…

> Packets of seed look dear in lists at a shilling each; I know now that they would be cheap at sixty… seed gathering is simply the most harrowing form of gambling as yet invented by humanity. All… are against you… all men, all beasts, all elements… At the end of ten days arduous trail… you arrive beneath your fifteen-thousand foot mountain on the guess that its seeds may be ready… Only to find they [the plants] never made any seed… it is not ripe… or… it is ripe and fallen… Or yaks trampled it.

Seed collecting continued apace but the question was how were they to obtain seed of the beautiful *Dipelta floribunda* they had seen earlier near the unfriendly Chago monastery, on the Tibetan side of the border, where their welcome remained uncertain. Even if accompanied by one of the donkey men, disguise was essential, but how was it to be done? Although enthusiastic to undertake the task, Farrer soon realised that 'gold teeth were not fashionable wear in Tibet… and their

*Purdom in disguise for collecting Dipelta, © and courtesy of the
Lakeland Horticultural Society*

blatant presence in the mouth of a labourer... certain to rouse unfavourable comment.'

So Purdom would go. With his moustache shaved, dressed in tatters and skin stained with burnt cork 'there now slouched the most villainous and magnificent labourer... a ruffian of daunting stature... The servants teetered in ecstasies at this transformation.' Although the monks were suspicious, the explanation that this disreputable character was the donkey-man's cousin, travelling to Szechuan to find a wife, was accepted. They had to work swiftly before they aroused too much suspicion and to Farrer's relief they returned exhausted but laden with seeds of the *Dipelta* and *Buddleia*.

By the middle of October the weather had turned bitterly cold and snow had started to fall as they returned once more to Siku, where an unwelcome surprise awaited them. Two other foreign plant collectors had arrived. It was Frank Meyer, with a Dutch colleague and an interpreter, travelling on behalf of the Agricultural Department of the American Government.

Purdom had met him before in England but Farrer was unconcerned, since Meyer had no interest in alpines. Farrer made a point of noting Meyer's dislike of the Chinese and the fact he had made no effort to learn even the basics of the language, despite being in China previously. Meyer had already travelled extensively and made major collections of fruiting trees and shrubs that would be successful in northern America. He could not have survived if it had been his habit to upset the local Chinese at every opportunity, as Farrer suggested.

It seemed, however, that Meyer was soon in difficulties. His interpreter refused to travel any further into unknown territory. An altercation followed and heedless of how much he needed Chinese help, Meyer not only ejected the interpreter but, according to Farrer, struck the labourer who tried to intervene. Farrer and Purdom had made particular efforts to remain on good terms with the governors and people of Siku, who instinctively distrusted foreigners of any kind. 'Rudeness or violence on the part of the foreigner' could only antagonise them.

Meyer was now unable to get any support. In an effort to help him, they arranged a meeting with the governor, but his impatience was such that the normal rules of courtesy were broken. Eventually some help was forthcoming, thanks to their good offices, but his expedition outside Siku was short-lived and he soon returned to make his way north to Lanchow.

As October came to an end, they decided to split up again. Farrer headed for Minchow while Purdom tried the mountains around Choni from where he returned, laden with seeds. It was now obvious that the exhausted Farrer could go no further on horseback. From Taochow onwards he would travel in the comparative comfort of a sedan chair, which was replaced by a cart, as they approached Lanchow.

They arrived on 20 November and although at first they stayed at an inn it soon became clear that a house would serve them better through the winter months, so that the drying and sorting of seeds could continue in earnest. Purdom set about the task of locating a suitable property with the help of the manager of the Post Office, a Yorkshireman. Over the next few days Purdom unloaded their baggage including 'a glorious and aged tripod which he had been given for a debt in Taochow'. While Farrer spent the evening working on his proofs, Purdom read newspapers and sewed on buttons.

The local officials entertained them in the evenings and said they thought the War in Europe was Armageddon. The drying and packing of seeds continued. As ever Farrer seemed inclined to neglect Fenwick Owen and Purdom could only look on and keep quiet. His main concern was to ensure Dr Hough received his fair share and so sent him more of his own collecting privately by separate post. By 25 November he had become unwell with a stomach upset, which left him pale and ill. As he grew worse remedies (nature unspecified) had to be obtained. He was also feeling increasingly guilty about not returning to enlist. Despite still being under the weather he had found them a house and, as soon as they moved in, began developing rolls of Farrer's films.

This peaceful interlude would not last. A letter which Dr Hough had written to the *Gardeners' Chronicle (*published 3 October) had just come to hand:

> It will interest many of your readers to know that Mr W. Purdom took an active part in organising the expedition and went to Peking some weeks ahead of Mr Farrer to have all in readiness... Mr Purdom has previously explored much of the ground... and any measure of success... will be largely due to the experience previously gained by him.

Farrer was enraged, insisted HE had organised the trip and that people should mind their own business. At one point he called Hough a silly owl. Other friends agreed with Hough and commented Purdom had been badly done by and that Farrer's reports to *The Gardeners' Chronicle* were noticeably one sided. Purdom could not intervene on behalf of his dear friend, but privately felt that Farrer's behaviour had been appalling and that he was proving a crashing snob. Perhaps this episode indicates how exhausted both men were. Tempers frayed easily.

At some stage Purdom must have confided to Farrer that he felt he had not been treated entirely fairly on the Veitch/Arnold Arboretum expedition and that

Mr Li and Mr Lo, © British Library Board

the collections he had made and which had nearly cost him his life were not appreciated. Purdom was prone to bouts of depression when worn out and clearly continued to feel bitter at being undervalued.

Just before Christmas Farrer wrote to Professor Balfour in Edinburgh with details of their achievements to date; the need to prepare their extensive harvest for despatch; their planned route for 1915 and in particular his assessment of Purdom. He had come to admire his qualities of resourcefulness and endurance and made it clear Purdom 'should get the very amplest credit out of this expedition'. In his third volume of their adventures *The Rainbow Bridge*, Farrer's comments were all generosity and kindness towards Purdom, now his valued travelling companion, who in this volume he would call Bill.

In all his correspondence on a personal or business level and in his publications in the *Gardeners' Chronicle,* the *Royal Horticultural Society Journal* and the *Geographical Journal* a different Farrer emerges both in style and character. The danger is in taking only one publication as an indication of Farrer's personality and failing to recognise that he could be generous to his friends as well as critical.

His article in the *Gardeners' Chronicle* of 27 February 1915 certainly suggests he was still upset: '

> by the well-meant but ill-judged letter... I call the expedition mine because it is
> – planned and arranged by me, and joined by Mr Purdom on my invitation... I
> did not see... any reason for making my published articles a puffing advertisement
> of either my companion or myself... I choose, if you please, my own time and
> methods for making something like an adequate acknowledgment of all that my
> expedition owes to this famous collector.

Over the winter a round of social activities ensued. All this delighted Farrer and his associating with the Chinese may well have been the reason for Meyer's sour comment that he and Purdom were somewhat out of order. With the help of Mr Li and Mr Lo (picture on page 99) from wealthy families in Canton, Farrer now embarked on a collecting spree of local treasures and artefacts. The only way to obtain the best was through personal introduction to private collections and these two exiles from Canton did know 'the best circles, spheres, lines, ranks, everything'.

At the end of January Purdom set off accompanied by two mounted soldiers, on a special mission to Choni, to obtain the precious Tibetan copperware that Farrer particularly desired. He would be away for over six weeks, returning in radiant health and good spirits. A few days after his return he operated on

Go-go's wisdom tooth and had started to smoke excessively, which worried Farrer.

Spring was a long time in coming and the Yellow River remained frozen. It was not until 28 March that they were able to leave Lanchow for Sining in the north-west. They were going to an area where only Przewalski had travelled before. The glowing Russian accounts had encouraged Farrer to believe it would produce as yet undiscovered novelties. However, it became obvious all too soon that the distant mountains were mainly of volcanic origin, not the limestone most suited to alpine plants.

Purdom, the City Governor and Farrer, © *British Library Board*

In Sining their inn proved so filthy it had to be cleaned thoroughly and the walls papered before it was fit to be occupied. Purdom then rode out to survey the surrounding country. He planned to travel fast and light and assured Farrer he would make better progress alone. Farrer waited for his return through the long and empty days, as he watched for any evidence that spring was on its way. Purdom returned towards the end of April in an exhausted state and disheartened to a degree. Travelling had proved hard; the land high and bare showed little prospect of success. The weather then closed in again with snow preventing any opportunity to leave. Even in early May little was in flower, although *Viburnum fragrans* was in bloom in pink and white forms in temple and private gardens.

While they waited for spring to arrive properly, invitations were received from the genial City Governor 'a stumpy little bowlered figure' and the Viceroy of Kansu 'a huge tall voluminous fellow' who insisted on changing into his military uniform for a photograph during the party he gave in their honour.

The frozen Hwang Hor, photograph © and courtesy of Royal Botanic Garden, Edinburgh, Farrer Archive.

At last they set out for the Da-tung Alps and in the clear air the mountains (some 17,000 feet) seeming tantalisingly close. Purdom again went ahead to get everything prepared for Farrer's arrival at their base for the summer, Wolvesden House.

Communications between Wolvesden and the outside world proved difficult. The Chinese post did not operate beyond Sining, so a local man was hired to carry letters and packages each way, perhaps once or twice a week. During this time Farrer continued to send regular reports to the *Gardeners' Chronicle*, but it could take at least six months before they appeared in print. Tibetan was now the main language spoken outside of administrative circles and their opium addicted interpreter was simply not up to the task.

The Viceroy of Kansu © *British Library Board*

As summer still delayed, they decided to move down to the warmer level of Tien Tang, where they arrived on 18 May. Their reception at the abbey was in complete contrast to the one they experienced at the hands of the lamas in Chago. Here they were welcomed; good accommodation provided for Purdom and the staff; while Farrer had his own rooms, from which he could see the altars and Buddhas of the abbey. Leaving Tien Tang they crossed high passes on their way to Chebson Abbey and the Da Tung Alps.

Purdom by this time had developed a raging tooth ache and all efforts – some of them eye-watering – to remove the tooth failed. There was nothing he could do but leave Chebson and make the weary journey back to Sining for more professional help, while Farrer continued collecting.

In early June the weather again turned cold, with snow falling on the mountain peaks; at 12,000 feet there was little sign of growth, so on Purdom's return, they prepared to leave Chebson and head back to Wolvesden, in a desperate attempt to find sheltered limestone valleys, more suited to alpine flora. The season advanced but despite the promising discovery of dolomite outcrops few, if any, alpine novelties were found. Purdom suggested it might be better to make for the higher levels and set up camp by the Clear Lake (Farrer's name for it). On 7 July they saw *Meconopsis quintuplinervia* in such abundance, that Farrer felt unable to

High Pass to Chebson, © and courtesy of the Lakeland Horticultural Society

William Purdom working on the screes, courtesy of Mrs. Joan Farrer.

describe adequately, despite the five pages he devoted to the experience.

Struggling with the effects of the high altitude, Farrer reluctantly admitted that they were too far north. Sadly the prevailing granite shingles, screes, ravines and cliffs were not going to be productive. The year was bound to end in failure. In an effort to retrieve the situation they agreed that Purdom should head for the Kokonor while Farrer completed the harvest in the alps before they met again at Wolvesden.

Camp at the Clear Lake, © and courtesy of the Lakeland Horticultural Society

Purdom returned from the Kokonor downcast at the lack of success. Everyone now succumbed to a flu-like illness. Quinine was of some help but Farrer resorted to his customary habit, when ill, of taking two pills of every variety in their Burroughs and Wellcome tabloid medicine chest. Exactly which box they had with them is uncertain; those taken by Scott to the Antarctic and Stanley to Africa contained such alarming concoctions as 'Forced March: a mixture of cocaine and caffeine designed to 'prolong the power of endurance' and 'Livingstone Rouser: a powerful laxative and expedition favourite.' The possibility that Farrer managed to combine these might explain his comment, that on this occasion, he realised he had overdone his selection and though an effect was produced it was almost excessive.

Wolvesden House, September 1915, © and courtesy of the
Lakeland Horticultural Society

Farrer described leaving his beloved Wolvesden for the last time, on a frosty and golden 13 September, as a dreadful experience.

Back in Lanchow, time passed quickly packing the specimens and the furs, bronzes and china (mainly Farrer's) onto three carts which would be taken down country to connect with the railway to Peking. Purdom, again travelling light, set off to collect any remaining seeds in the Choni area, while Farrer headed south by horse litter to the Szechuan border. By 17 October he had arrived in Loyang, where he waited anxiously for Purdom.

The final stages of their journey were by river, firstly on *The Ark* down a tributary of the Yangste to Chung King, then by steamer through the gorges to Ichang where they arrived on 29 November. Farrer called this day 'the bitter end

The Ark, © and courtesy of the Lakeland Horticultural Society

of all things'. All that remained was the long rail journey to Peking

The tone of *The Rainbow Bridge* recording their adventures in 1915 is often darker than that of the two earlier volumes. By the time it was written in 1918 Farrer had experienced at first hand the horrors of the First World War, while acting as war correspondent to John Buchan. He apologised to his readers, explaining that he was 'writing this book for the release of one person only... I am strenuously re-living, in fact, the dead years, in order to win free a while from the present; ...Spinning a rainbow bridge, far-flung over the black depths, towards the golden irrecoverable past.'

9

Staying On

Arriving in Peking on 6 December 1915, they must have been exhausted and Farrer remembered the pleasure of the first real bath he'd had for almost two years. Purdom was again involved with the practicalities of organising all the baggage but Farrer was not idle. He had three months correspondence waiting for him, people to meet and acquaintances to renew.

Barely a week had passed before Farrer wrote to his mother that Purdom had at last secured, what appeared to be, his dream job. Of course, it was all through Farrer's good offices that such excellent terms were arranged. He explained that Purdom being,

so soft and amenable that I [Farrer] had to insert protective clauses and stand out for terms!… Nothing could possibly have turned out better and I do feel delighted in having been half a means – even of helping him to such an eminently suitable job, as a sort of vicarious part payment for his two years of indefatigable charmingness and good fellowship in my perfectly unpaid service.*

Purdom had been appointed an Imperial Forestry Commissioner, on a three year contract, by Mr Chow Tze-chi, at a salary of £800 a year plus expenses. His brief was to organise the afforestation of Northern China, travelling extensively to source suitable trees and set up vast propagation nurseries.

Farrer had secured Purdom a month's preliminary holiday prior to taking up the new position. This time was spent in packing and preparing for despatch all the remaining seeds, boxes and curios they had amassed during the expedition.

They had also been in touch with Morrison. Farrer (it appears without Purdom being invited) enjoying a Christmas party, to which he arrived late and had to

---

* From letter Farrer sent to his mother on 14 December 1915, courtesy of Mrs Joan Farrer.

apologise profusely as a result. In return he invited Morrison and his wife to his modest 'Casa Mia' for tea and to see his sketches and photographs of China and Tibet.

Purdom had intended to return to England at the end of the Kansu Expedition. If the Forestry position had not arisen he probably would have done so, although the temptation to remain in China, and achieve something for the Empire, was strong.

By the beginning of March Purdom was established in his new position, travelling north to Tientsin and then back to Peking, to assess how existing nurseries were administered and reviewing possible future staff. He was asked by the Governor of the TPR (Tientsin Peking Railway?) nursery about his superior Forsythe Sherfesee, an American who had worked for ten years as Director of Forestry in the Philippines before joining the Bureau of Forestry in China in 1916. He wanted to know about Sherfesee's work experience, his opinions and above all his loyalty.

Farrer planned to return home in April via the Trans-Siberian railway, which would give him the opportunity to stop at St Petersburg and visit the botanic archives there. Although unrest was simmering in Russia there would still be a few months of relative calm before full revolution broke out.

Purdom had made an appointment to meet Morrison on 8 April but had been asked, at very short notice, to give a talk to the Forest Service Club instead, which the Minister (unspecified) was going to attend. The tone of his apology was cordial and there was no hint of the storm clouds about to gather.

On 17 April 1916, Farrer wrote his farewell letter to Morrison, thanking him for his friendliness and promising him a copy of the book as soon as it was published.

There then follows an extraordinary passage in which he expresses his concern for Purdom,

his one day of leisure is now almost always commandeered by people who seem to think that here's a fine chance of getting a first-class gardener for nothing! – I was particularly pleased to hear, though that he'd been planting for you the other day – as I know he will have enjoyed this.

Apparently someone had claimed Purdom owed his job to him and that it was reasonable to expect him to work for nothing to pay off that debt. Farrer, of course, had no idea who the person was but suspected it must be 'some peculiarly underbred woman'. It was also a pity that Purdom had only been given a secondary position, as the principal post had been taken up by a pro-German American, 'perpetually hob-nobbing with the German Minister' with the intention of ensuring a German foothold in China. The letter ended in the most cordial way in the hope they might meet in London in the not too distant future.

What did Farrer intend? He seemed genuinely concerned that Purdom was being put upon and asked Morrison to continue to keep a friendly eye on him. Whatever Farrer's intention, Morrison's reply on 19 April was incandescent,

> Rarely have I received a more offensive communication, with its cheap sarcasm and insulting insinuation… Made still more odious by your action in arranging that it should reach me only after your departure.

Morrison's counterclaim was that *he* had helped Purdom to obtain the position. *He* had done this at Purdom's request after he had heard about their journey together and how appallingly Farrer had behaved and exploited him. Yes, he had allowed him to use a small plot of land to cultivate the seeds he had collected and hoped to sell for a profit – just as Farrer intended to do with his collection when he returned to London. According to Morrison, it was clear that Farrer himself had been running Purdom into the ground,

> It is true I did not tip him… If Purdom has been overworked, it is you who have overworked him… In England he would have to work with his hands, and would be paid a comparatively small weekly wage.

He then proceeded to condemn his erstwhile friend; Purdom did not get the senior position because he was not capable of doing it and by traducing the good name of his Department Chief had made a bad beginning.

Morrison lost no time in sending a copy of Farrer's offending letter to Purdom demanding an explanation, as Farrer's complete misrepresentation of the facts could only have come from Purdom himself. On returning from Kansu, Purdom had complained bitterly to him about Farrer and described him as a freak, with a liking for the bottle, especially when they passed the winter in Lanchow.

From his early days in Peking Morrison was in the habit of recording gossip and rumour in his diary, in case they might be useful at a later date. He made it clear he would not let any of Purdom's spurious claims affect his rapport with Farrer, whom he said he liked and who would always be welcome in his home. This seems a bizarre stance given the outrage in his previous letter to Farrer. Purdom had clearly made unwise and unguarded comments to Morrison, believing him to be a friend and confidant; but careful notes of their meeting on 18 December appear to have been kept for Morrison to recall them in such detail.

So within three short weeks the cordial relations that had existed between Morrison and Purdom changed dramatically: 'My dear Doctor' was reduced to 'Dear Sir' and followed by a complete denial of all the points in Morrison's letter. Purdom was not prepared to answer or stand for anything Farrer had said or written.

Given the febrile atmosphere in Peking at this time, with the First World War now in its second year, feelings would have been running high. It was the Chinese who had first expressed concerns about Sherfesee and Purdom was already aware that something was seriously amiss at the Forestry Commission. He had been warned by his Chinese friends that forces there were plotting against him. Whatever the truth of the matter Purdom was extremely worried about the War and convinced that guns and shells were not the way to solve disagreements. It was his duty to return home, but the authorities in China made it clear to him that any vacant post would be filled by Germans. Shortly after Farrer left he had handed in his three month notice and on 4 May sent a telegram saying he was coming home and could Madge be advised.

But Farrer had not yet finished with Morrison, (whose registered letter had finally arrived in England) and on 14 May, replied,

I wrote to you [I] commended the victim [Purdom] to your good offices. You reply, passionately claiming the discredit for yourself... in three pages... conveyed with the crudest incivility of expression!! The rest of your letter... asks for the charity of oblivion... I know Purdom too well to believe you well-inspired in the colouring you try to put on our relations.

Farrer, of course, could speak and write as freely as he pleased. His family was wealthy and he was financially independent. Purdom would never have that freedom and could not afford to upset powerful men, especially one like Morrison who could prove vindictive and whose attitude towards Purdom was inconsistent.

The highly complex and unstable political situation in China did not help. Yuan Shih-k'ai had been proclaimed Emperor on 22 December 1915 and then stood down in March 1916 to become President again. Who was actually in control of the administration of governmental departments was constantly changing. Following the death of Yuan in June 1916, the Forestry Service was abolished and all responsibilities taken over by the Ministry of Agriculture. Staff had not been paid. Purdom was obliged to let his house and move to an inn with a Chinese friend. His three month notice had not been accepted and so months passed with virtually nothing to do. He felt it was like being in a prison and ached to be back in the mountains. He was still in Peking at the end of the year.

In December he wrote to Farrer, on Ministry of Agriculture and Commerce paper, explaining the specimens he had promised to despatch continued to be delayed by a shipping strike along the coast. He had checked them every month for worm and moth damage and repacked them in Legation boxes ready to go. A new route would be tried via the Cape to London in the hope they would arrive safely and pass through customs without incident. However, he felt unable to visit the Legation personally at this time since there seemed some question of arousing suspicion, if he were seen there too often. What he meant by this is unclear. He noted with sadness the death of one of Farrer's friends from Baliol days; Raymond Asquith had died in France in September.

Purdom had been so relieved when Farrer, full of himself as ever, left Peking; then there was the debacle of the Morrison letters. Yet at the end of 1916 he is writing to Farrer with an unexpected degree of warmth. Perhaps the preceding lonely and frustrating six months had softened his opinion.

Meyer was still collecting in China at this time and seemed unaware of the changing situation in Peking. The rumoured salaries of Sherfesee and Purdom still rankled with him and the tone of his letters suggested he felt the sums were completely undeserved. Reporting back to Fairchild in America, he repeated the salaries in Mexican silver and US gold and seemed to enjoy telling another correspondent that Farrer's new book would be very disappointing as the expedition was known to be a failure. Morrison would make similar comments about Purdom's imagined earnings. Morrison considered, after all the work he had done for *The Times* he had been badly paid and had returned home, in his terms a poor man, after selling his book collection for a mere £35,000.

By 1917 Farrer was working in France as a war correspondent for John Buchan, writing from Arras, the Somme, Ypres, Thiepval, Lens and Vimy before going on to Italy. His book *The Void of War* is chilling in its detachment and all the more telling through its understatement. Of a soldier newly arrived at Vimy Ridge, who just wanted to talk to *someone* – even his superior officer (although that was against the rules), he wrote, 'He knew, and we knew ourselves, that in a few days he would almost certainly be dead.'

The day after his birthday on 10 April, and somewhat the worse for wear, Purdom wrote to thank Farrer for the many notes he had sent and the copies of the *Royal Geographical Journal* in which Farrer had mentioned him. He continued to live on the west side of Peking with his Chinese friends, rather than in the east where the majority of foreigners were.

Although he had no real interest in their gossip or intrigues he had been delighted to attend Arbor Day at the Temple of Heaven on the 5 April, saying all the Chinese 'K'nuts' went. This curious term was coined in 1911 from the popular song *Gilbert the Filbert* and subsequently much used to denote idle, upper class, men-about-town,

> *I'm Gilbert the Filbert the Knut with a K,*
> *The pride of Piccadilly the blasé roué,*
> *Oh Hades, the ladies, who leave their wooden huts,*
> *For Gilbert the Filbert the Colonel of the Knuts.*

Describing himself as 'seductive Bill' he regaled Farrer with details of a few of their past acquaintances including a Mrs Barton who gushed 'OH, MR PURDOM … MR PURDOM what a long time it is since we met' with much rolling of her eyes; a Miss Price had 'chucked' her fiancé in favour of a naval commander and more; 'everything is private until the seventh cocktail'.

His sister Nell had also been in touch with Farrer and they were both clearly concerned about him, believing a life of solitude did not agree with his nerves or his health. Although Nell was 28 and had been a teacher for at least seven years, to travel to China in the midst of the War and while the Russian Revolution was raging, took some courage. With over 700,000 rail workers on strike in Russia, travelling on the Trans-Siberian route was out of the question. The sea was far from safe; the *Lusitania* had been torpedoed in 1915 with the loss of over 1,000 lives. The route Nell took is unknown but she arrived in Tientsin in 1917 at about the time of the Moon Festival. This would have been towards the end of September or early October. Purdom was there to meet her from the ship and take her to the apartment he had rented (Kan Shih Chiao – Sweet Stone Bridge), in part of a former Manchu palace, in the western district of Peking.

Screen at entrance to Kan Shih Chiao by William Purdom,
©The Royal Geographic Society

One of Nell's first tasks was to learn how to use the telephone in case she needed to contact William at the Ministry of Agriculture. Mastering the different Chinese tones was just like practising the scales he said... so up and down she went through the numbers from one to ten. Living next door was a Duke from the Manchu court, who attended the young Emperor every day in the Imperial City. It was a curious arrangement. The president Yuan Shih-k'ai, who held the reins of power, used to sign state papers in a modest office, while the Emperor lived in luxury surrounded by a huge staff of retainers.

The Duke and Duchess were to prove genial neighbours. The Duchess had invited them both to a feast to celebrate the mid-autumn festival. Nell needed to understand the complexities of Chinese etiquette as swiftly as possible. Using chopsticks correctly to cope with the thirty different dishes on the menu was a priority. She started practising by picking up beads from a plate. Generally William and Nell avoided contact with other westerners but they did have a few close

Purdom with Mr Han, © and courtesy of the Lakeland Horticultural Society

English friends with whom they passed Christmas and New Year. Nell gradually gained confidence and offered English lessons to several Chinese girls.

Nell described this time spent with her brother as magical; horse riding in the mornings; visiting the city by rickshaw; ice skating; wrapped up in furs and felt to go on a winter picnic by sledge along the frozen canal. She learned to speak Chinese and practised writing with a tutor who claimed his seven year old son already recognised 7,000 characters.

One of the most poignant moments was one evening when William took her to the top of the Great Wall overlooking the city. Holding her hand he asked her to keep her eyes shut and quoted the words their family always used when giving them presents, 'Close your eyes and see what God will send you'. In the sunset the autumn trees, gilded roofs of the palaces and lakes glowed, as if in a fairy tale.

Nell stayed in Peking for almost a year. Writing to Farrer in April 1918, she spoke of her deep affection for 'Billiam… he being the most adorable old thing to me'. She was relieved that at last he seemed to have some practical work to do. Their Chinese friends were as supportive to her as they could be, but when he had been away for almost a month, she felt unspeakably lonely. She thought he would

Trip along branch line to Hsi Ling tombs, © and courtesy of the
Lakeland Horticultural Society

Rail carriage at Kouchuan, © and courtesy of the Lakeland Horticultural Society

come home if his situation remained unresolved and did 'not give him the opportunities to do his bit for Britain' in China. The end of the War seemed so far away.

From March 1918 until his return to Peking in early April Purdom travelled widely, with colleagues Mr Han and Mr Long. They went north to Tientsin and then turned south with the intention of seeing the Kunshan Forest Station, near Shanghai. However, the trains could not stop there due to an outbreak of plague, so they continued to Nanking.

Although Purdom was making notes of the trees, soil conditions, climate and the suitability of each area for developing tree nurseries, he also described the trials of the journey, crowded trains, weary waits for ferries and people met along the way. Near Nanking they stayed at an inn 'more of the brothel than hotel' before viewing the university nursery. Here they met a Professor Woodward 'a mouldy old mosquito eaten old devil... with whiskers hanging down like grey fungus.' Although the nursery was poorly managed he was impressed by the comfortable accommodation provided for the staff.

He later visited the nearby Hsi Ling Tombs and a temple which he described

Kwang Shan Po hilltop office, © and courtesy of the Lakeland Horticultural Society.

as quite the prettiest he had seen. After returning to Peking, he spent most of June working along the Canton Hankow Railway. Locations were marked by numbered milestones. The weather varied between heavy rain and hot spells; there were millions of mosquitoes.

Establishing or developing existing nurseries was a major task. Trees were desperately needed for the extension of the Chinese railway system and also for the afforestation project. Purdom travelled the length of various railway lines. Sometimes he was fortunate to stay at inns but for a considerable time simply lived in a rail carriage.

The Kwang (Hwang) Shan Po Forest Station was the largest on the Kin Han Line, its office built among trees on a hillside with seed beds in the nursery and villages nearby.

He described Li Kia Chia as one of the most favourable forest sites on the Kin Han Railway and one directly controlled by him. He was also continuing his work with the nurseries along the Hankow Line.

By the time First World War ended in November 1918 Farrer was already planning another expedition, this time to Upper Burma. He had hoped to persuade Purdom to take part, as he had relied on him so much to manage people and organise everything. Purdom regretted he could not leave his position in China and Farrer was faced with doing everything for himself and possibly travelling alone. He set off in January 1919 with Euan Cox as his companion for the first year.

In the spring of 1920 Farrer must have sent Purdom a questionnaire or plan for setting up a business 'Eyebright and Co.' in China, based on making and retailing a form of cosmetic salve. He had asked if Purdom would like to take a

Scenes at railway station during the famine of 1920, © and courtesy of the Lakeland Horticultural Society

share in the company. On 20 June Purdom wrote to explain he didn't want to discourage Farrer completely but any thought of commercial travelling into the interior was completely out of the question; the countryside was divided into what were effectively little kingdoms, each under the control of a different faction. Not even the railways were safe; trains were held up by robbers; the passengers relieved of all their valuables or forced to walk to another waiting train under the control of yet another lawless band. Cox must also have been involved as Purdom sent him a copy of

Courtesy of Mrs. Lorraine Crook.

his long and detailed reply. He advised holding off for a while, until the financial and political situation was more settled.

Nonetheless he hoped Farrer was keeping well and that the expedition was proving successful. Perhaps they might meet in Peking before the end of the year. Thankfully he was in better health, having been unwell for six months in the previous year and looked forward to receiving the next instalments of *The Eaves of the World*.

At almost the same time Farrer had written to Aubrey Herbert about the isolation and difficult conditions he was experiencing in Burma. The torrential rains, savage mountains and impenetrable jungle were a nightmare. He expected to stay in Burma for another year and return home via Peking in 1921. In his last letter to Herbert, he invited him to come out to Burma and share the journey back. He had decided at the grand age of 40 it was time to settle down 'do my duty and get wed. Find me a fair one please... Against all evidence I hope by now that I am... less selfish and silly than I've always been... Anyhow there it is: a serious intention and a definite request.'

Sadly none of Farrer's dreams or plans for the future or another expedition (realistic or otherwise) would come true. He died on 17 October 1920, at Nyitadi on the Burma/China border, possibly of a chest infection; diphtheria has been suggested.

The details of Purdom's six month illness in 1919 are unknown. He had always had a tendency to overwork and travelling and living conditions were a trial. The drought of 1919, particularly in the northern provinces, had caused the failure of the rice crop and subsequently led to the famine of 1920. He witnessed at first hand the suffering of the Chinese at this time.

In 1920 his services to the Chinese Board of Agriculture were recognised by the gift of a silver cup and diploma *'in recognition of his superior skill'*.

In the following year he took on responsibility for a comprehensive survey for the railways of China, as forestry officer and also as supervisor for the supply of wood for the railways. This placed a further strain on his health.

Towards the end of October he was taken to the French hospital in Peking for what was described as a minor operation on an infected gland in his neck. During his first expedition in 1909 he had previously suffered from two large abscesses on his neck, which he put down to the poor water supply. Whether the operation itself was successful or not he then developed 'chronic rheumatism, affecting the heart and pneumonia.'

It is possible he suffered from a septic throat infection after the operation and heart failure followed. Antibiotics had yet to be discovered. Whatever the precise cause of the 'rheumatism' he died only two weeks later on 7 November 1921.

It is to be hoped that Nell managed to reach Peking in time to be with him as she was teaching in Kuling at the time. According to the *The Westmorland Gazette* of 19 November a telegram with the sad news of his death was sent to their parents in Brathay and it named Miss M. Purdom as the sender. It seems unlikely that Margaret could have travelled to Peking so quickly but Nell might have sent her the telegram.

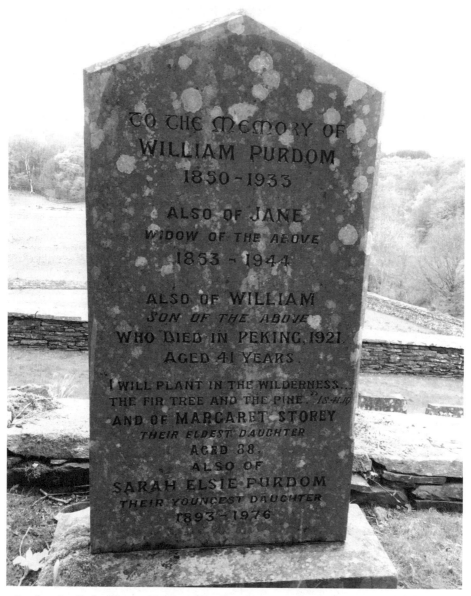

Purdom family headstone Brathay Church, author's photograph. Quotation: a part of Isaiah 41:19 "I will plant in the wilderness the fir tree and the pine."

Purdom had largely shunned the European enclave in Peking, preferring to live on the west side with his Chinese friends. Although in his last few years he was away from Peking for much of the time, he was still known to the European community. His obituary in the *Journal of the Kew Guild* stresses the hardships he endured; living on a rail car, not being paid and coping with many changes in Government, 'but our late friend loved his work and kept England's prestige high'. It includes a poem by Lady Clifton written from the British Legation in Peking.

Memorial stone photographs courtesy of the British Embassy, Beijing.

A Perfect Friend: William Purdom

...This man, more rare, did spend his strength and mind
Outside an office, trod no barrack square
But made of trees his textbooks, and did find
Much good in flowers...

He is commemorated on the family gravestone in Brathay churchyard.

Exactly where he was buried is uncertain, though one source suggests the British Cemetery in the XiBianMen district of today's Beijing. A stone memorial to him was erected in the British Legation Quarter but was subsequently moved to the grounds of the British Embassy. Inscriptions on its sides are from Lady Clifton's poem; the carving on the top, now almost completely worn away, gives his name as 'botanist'.

The lack of personal or family records, means that Purdom's personality remains elusive. All that is left is a series of what might be called cameos – how Purdom was seen through the eyes of others.

However, perhaps it is time to review the constantly repeated description of him as 'tall and lean, of magnificent Nordic physique; equable and reticent'; surely a biographer's dream. It is with some sadness that such fond imaginings must be cast aside.

Purdom was average height at 5' 9" and at times rather stout. He could certainly be reticent and equable if he wished, but whether Sir William Thiselton-Dyer would have agreed, after their confrontations at Kew, is open to question.

In professional terms he was always described as a hard worker, perhaps inclined to overwork. His skills as a hardwood propagator were second to none. Given his union activities at Kew he would not have had the continued support of the management, if his work had been lax. He could be obtuse and almost his own worst enemy; Colonel Prain had to go to extraordinary lengths to help him without his realising it. On the other hand, it was his integrity and genuine concern for the well-being of others that caused him to take a stand against what he viewed as unfairness and unacceptable social inequalities.

Farrer understood him so well and when writing to Professor Balfour mentioned Purdom's future. Farrer described him as being of a fiery loyalty, devoted to the needs of others and not possessed of the 'supple knee and neck that some 'great men' demand'. What Purdom needed was a situation where he could

William Purdom, © British Library Board

vote Liberal and where 'all crossing sweepers had a fair living wage'.

Despite his courage in standing up for others, he clearly had periods of self-doubt, verging on depression. He could be overwhelmed by the feeling that he had done his utmost, had failed, that others were to blame and at times appeared to have a chip on his shoulder. The problem was that life in the early 1900s was not fair to aspiring workers from the lower orders.

And yet he had an engaging side to his character that endeared him to many. As a youth he had enjoyed acting in local plays; his sister Nell remembered vividly his gift for mimicry which enabled him to learn Chinese easily and carry on 'laughing talk' with his staff and muleteers. He had the rare ability to gain the trust and loyalty of the Chinese he met and whom he always described and thought of as his friends. His mentor and close friend Charles Hough described as a 'dear man with whom it was a privilege to claim friendship'.

He shared a sense of the ridiculous with Farrer, whose 'leg-pulling' he greatly missed in the later years. To Farrer he was simply 'a perfect friend'.

Then he was almost forgotten but not quite…

10

Forgotten and Remembered

Apart from the occasional entry in horticultural publications Purdom's name faded from sight. Of course the family mourned but no one had seen him, apart from Nell, for over seven years. All the other children had left home, with the exception of Elsie. These two sisters kept William's memory alive between them. Nell in her recollections about her time in Beijing and Elsie with the mementos she kept of his travels. A sword given to him for his protection hung over the mantelpiece at Brathay Lodge. Both Nell and Elsie died without children and here his story might have ended.

Near Xinyang in the province of Henan is Jigongshan (Rooster Mountain). For about 30 years from the end of the nineteenth century villas were built in the area for foreign missionaries and subsequently Chinese officials. It became a famous resort to escape the summer heat.

The scenery is very like Purdom's native Lake District, though on a grander scale with rolling wooded hills and mountains. In 1918 Purdom and Han An, arrived here to establish a nursery; a project so dear to Purdom's heart – the planting of trees. In the following years, they introduced several species mainly from North America in particular *Taxodium*

Sword given by Aco-che-ro to William Palmer for his own protection. Photograph © and courtesy of the Lakeland Horticultural Society.

distichum and *Taxodium ascendens* which would provide valuable timber for the railways.

Despite all the hardships he experienced Purdom was not always alone. The photograph opposite shows the 'guardian' of the Jigongshan nursery and his children. The photograph on page 132 shows what appears to be the same dog, the same children (i.e. the guardian's) and Purdom looking very relaxed. It is believed he had a Chinese girlfriend but never married.

In August 2006 news came that in the Jigongshan National Park, a Purdom Memorial Forest Park and Museum had been opened. The park contains the spectacular stands of *Taxodium*; streams and lakes. Locally the park is valued for the thousand or more species of flora and fauna, which has earned it the titles of 'Wildlife Gene Pool' and 'Nature Treasure Bowl'. The museum contains a series

Rooster mountain station

The Rooster Mountain Station guardian with family – Chi Kung shan [sic].
Photograph © and courtesy of the Lakeland Horticultural Society.

Purdom with Chinese family. Photograph © and courtesy of Cumbria Archive Services.

of panels illustrating Purdom's life and Mr Han An, and their work together developing the tree nurseries. In 1922 a memorial was erected there in Purdom's memory.

It is a great honour for Purdom to be remembered and commemorated in this way. The mutual friendship and respect he shared with the Chinese people remains a shining example to this day.

Above Jigongshan and below the view from Jigongshan.

The Purdom Forest Park Official Opening. These colour photographs were either sent to the author, who was unable to attend the official opening or were taken during a memorable visit in 2008. The kindness of everyone involved has never been forgotten.

Scenes within the Purdom Forest Park.

*Left, the Purdom Memorial and
below the Museum*

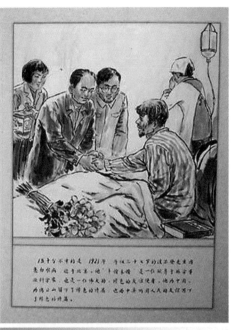

Illustrations in the Museum.

11

The Plants

Why are the plants only included in the last chapter of this book; after all Purdom and Farrer risked their lives to collect them?

Many of Purdom's plants were never identified and locating the herbarium samples, (let alone listing them) is a project beyond the scope of this current book. In addition today plant names are changing in the light of modern scientific knowledge.

For the amateur gardener this can prove bewildering. Obtaining the correct plant for a collection is fraught with difficulty; having finally tracked down a plant after many years searching and been assured 'it's the real thing', the amateur may well find experts disagreeing as to its precise identity or whether it exists at all. When it comes to recognising a collector as the person who introduced the plant another problem arises; in botanical terms *collected* and *introduced* are not necessarily synonymous.

Take *Viburnum fragans (farreri)* as an example. In his book *Trees and Shrubs Hardy in the British Isles* W. J. Bean describes it thus:

> Native of Kansu... First introduced by W. Purdom for Messrs. Veitch under his numbers 689 (white flowers) and 690 (pink). The first flowers I saw were sent to me from Wakehurst, Sussex, in March 1920, which had been gathered from one of Purdom's plants obtained from the Coombe Wood Nursery previously.

Purdom's herbarium sample of *Viburnum fragrans P690*, held at Kew is clearly marked 'temple Minchow'. This means that it could be regarded as cultivated stock. Farrer made a great point of explaining that Purdom showed him plants 'growing in the wild'. The new name *Viburnum farreri* was chosen by William Stearn in *Taxon* (1966) to commemorate Farrer.

Rhododendron purdomii has a story of its own. Some experts have said it does not exist at all but is just a minor variation of another form; others believe that given its provenance and botanical characteristics it can be called *Rhododendron purdomii*. The one that grew for many years at the Lakeland Horticultural Society came directly from the Brathay Lodge garden. Miss Elsie Purdom donated this to the Society before she died in 1976 because she had been unable to find one grown by any nursery. As it lost vigour in later years it struggled to survive the many attempts to propagate it either by cuttings or air layering; the parent branch would slowly die back as a result. Added to which honey fungus was becoming rampant in nearby beds. It eventually died some ten years ago. There seems to have been one other possible *Rhododendron purdomii* growing locally. This looked to be the same age and had been planted just inside the entrance to Brathay Church but appears to have been removed with other shrubs during the renovation of access to the church and its car park.

The identification of the Moutan peony is in a class of its own and still the subject of fierce debate. In 1990 in their review of *Paeonia suffruiticosa* (Edin.J.Bot. 47(3): 273-281) Messrs Haw and Lauener wrote:

'The first Westerner to find plants of *P. suffruticosa* growing in the wild was almost certainly William Purdom.' His number P338 collected '50 li west of Yenan-fu, Shensi' in the form of roots was identified as *Paeonia suffruticosa var spontanea* and the one collected on Tai Pei Shan as a form of *P. rockii*.

One of Purdom's favourite trees was *Betula albosinensis v. septentrionalis* (P.752) which he often described:

...you will be interested to hear I found the pretty Betula at Tai-pei-shan with the striking rosy bark which peels off like paper... The rosy red barked Betula was also growing out in Tibetan country, the Tibetans use the bark for wrapping their butter.

Purdom was completely overshadowed and understandably so by the success of George Forrest working in Yunnan and Ernest Wilson collecting for Veitch in more favourable areas such as Szechuan. Even then, Veitch was unable to ensure all Wilson's plants were identified correctly. The pending closure of the Veitch Nurseries meant that much of the Chinese stock was offered in dispersal sales.

Between 1913 and 1917 the Arnold Arboretum published the major work *Plantae Wilsonianae*, which listed not only Wilson's vast collection but a good proportion of Purdom's and that of other collectors. *The Journal of the Arnold Arboretum* (1922 Vol3 pp55-6) reported that he had sent 550 packets of seeds of trees and shrubs and that in the Arboretum Herbarium there were 'specimens collected by Purdom under eleven hundred numbers.'

Quite what happened to Purdom's other herbarium specimens is a little hazy. Some were sent by the Arnold Arboretum (duplicates) to the Smithsonian Institute, Berlin and other herbariums. The ones at Kew are searchable by plant name only (not collector), so how many they received from the Arnold Arboretum is uncertain; certainly others came directly from Veitch. A selection of 300 of Purdom's specimens was sent to the Royal Botanic Garden, Edinburgh, on 31 March 1921, in a consignment including collections by Simeon Ten (Yunnan) and Ernest Wilson (Formosa and Korea).

Most of the sponsors of the Farrer/Purdom expedition of 1914-15 received their allocation via Farrer's gardener Mr Redman at Clapham, although Purdom made a point of sending extra packets to Dr Hough at White Craggs whenever he could. In his book *A Westmorland Rock Garden* Dr Hough wrote how the packages of seeds arrived with careful notes of what they were, how they grew and where best to plant them at White Craggs.

Before the first allocation of seeds arrived the First World War had begun and the Hough family were variously committed to war work. There was not a man about the place to help them handle the seeds as so many had already left to serve in the War. Their share was about ten per cent and whenever they had spare time they would sort, weigh and divide this with the other local sponsors. The family would sit around the dining room table, scarcely daring to breathe in case they blew the precious seeds away. One daughter described it as rather fun, despite the anxiety.

Of course there could have been a wider variety of seeds but Farrer would not collect anything he deemed unworthy. He was determined to concentrate his efforts on the best that could be found. By doing this perhaps unusual but unlovely rarities were missed.

Some of the samples from Kansu Expedition with Farrer already appear online on the Herbarium website of the Royal Botanic Gardens, Edinburgh. At one time Farrer seemed amenable to both his and Purdom's name appearing on the attribution. He later suggested to Professor Balfour in Edinburgh that the majority should appear under his name only as he had organised the expedition.

The list below is based on *Plantae Wilsonianae* and various contemporary publications such as *The Gardeners' Chronicle, The Journal of the Arnold Arboretum (Arnoldia)*, herbarium samples or handwritten herbarium or seed lists (often by name and number only). In some cases the same number has been used more than once. The reason for this is unclear but possibly due to the loss of his field notes. Where possible the location and year have been included. Only the names found in the 2017 RHS Plantfinder have been included in this table.

Purdom's Expedition 1909-12

NAME	LOCATION	DATE	No.
Abelia biflora	Shansi, Wutai-shan	1909	297
Abies fargesii	Shensi Tai-pei-shan	1910	405
Abies nephrolepsis	Shansi, Wutai-shan	1909	141
Abies sibirica	Shansi, Wutai-shan	1909	143
Acer maximowiczii			947/948
Acer davidii			949
Actinidia chinensis			657
Adenophera polymorpha		1910	166
Aesculus chinensis	In the Western Hills, near Peking	1912	874
Albizia julibrissin			957
Arundinaria nitida	Shensi Tai-pei-shan	1910	980
Aster albescens	Kansu, Lotani on road to Siku		1088
Berberis amurensis			34
Berberis gilgiana	Shensi, Tai-pei-shan	1910	6, 7, 8
Berberis julianae	Shensi, Tai-pei-shan	1910	7
Berberis poiretii	Chihli East of Weichang	1909	
Berberis soulieana	Shensi, Tai-pei-shan	1910	7
Betula albosinensis v. septentrionalis	Kansu, Tao river district,	1911	752
Betula chinensis	N.Chihli ,Weichang (cuttings)	1909	85
Betula fruticosa	N. Chihli, C.& W. Weichang	1910	104
Buxus microphylla v. sinica	Shensi, Tai-pei-shan	1910	
Campanula punctata	N. Chihli, Weichang,	1909	41
Carpinus turczanowii	W. Kansu, Lotani	1911	787
Caryopteris incana	W. Kansu		792
Cercidiphyllum japonicum	Shensi, Tai-pei-shan, S. slopes	1910	1107

Chionanthus retusus	W.Kansu, Taochow		363
Clematis aethusifolia	Shansi, Wutai-shan	1910	180
Clematis alpina	Shansi, Wutai-shan	1910	149
Clematis fargesii v.souliei	Shensi, Tai-pei-shan	1910	540
Clematis macropetala	Shensi, Tai-pei-shan	1910	417a
Clematis tangutica v. obtusiuscula	W.Kansu, Choni & Taochow	1911	1023
Cortusa matthioli		1910	
Corylus heterophylla	N.Chihli, Weichang	1909	33
Corylus tibetica	Shensi, Tai-pei-shan	1910	457
Cotoneaster adpressus	W. Kansu, Taochow		1033
Cotoneaster gracilis	Shensi,Tai-pei-shan	1910	
Cotoneaster zabelii	Shensi, N.W.Hancheng-hsien	1910	360
Crataegus pinnatifolia		1909	57
Daphne giraldii	W.Kansu. West of Tow River		1083
Decaisnea fargesii	Shensi. Tai-pei-shan	1910	501
Deutzia grandiflora	Chihli, Weichang	1910	16/1068
Deutzia parviflora	Chili.Weichang	1910	40 & a
Deutzia rubens	Shensi, Tai-pei-shan	1910	428/581/662
Dracocephalum ruyschiana	N. Chihli, Weichang	1909	140
Eleagnus umbellata	W.Kansu, Choni	1912	336
Euonymous alatus	Shensi, Tai-pei-shan	1910	
Euonymous alatus	Shensi, N.W. Hancheng-hsien	1910	375
Euonymous alatus	Shensi,Yenan Fu	1910	342
Euonymus alatus	N.Chihli, Weichang	1909	30
Euonymus sanguinea	Shensi, Tai-pei-shan	1910	13
Euptelea pleiosperma	Shensi, Tai-pei-shan	1910	1036
Exochorda racemose v. giraldii	Shensi, Hancheng-hsien	1910	361
Hallenia elliptica		1911	466
Hippophae rhamnoides	Shansi, Wutai-shan		189
Hydrangea longipes			977
Indigofera amblyantha	Kansu	1911	539a

Indigofera pendula	W. Kansu		951
Juglans mandschurica	N. Chihli, Weichang	1909	90
Juniperus chinensis	Shensi, base of Tai-pei-shan	1910	
Larix principis-ruprechtii	Shansi, Wutai village		161
Leptodermis oblonga	North China, no precise locality		319 & a
Lespedeza bicolor	Chihli, Weichang	1909	123
Ligularia stenocephala	Shansi, Wutai-shan	1910	172
Lonicera chaetocarpa	Shensi, Tai-pei-shan	1910	391
Lonicera hispida	Shensi, Tai-pei-shan	1910	391a
Lonicera maackii			371
Lonicera syringantha	W.Kansu, Choni	1911	699
Malus baccata	Shensi, Yenan Fu	1910	329
Malus kansuensis	W.Kansu,Tibetan country, S. Tao river	1910	1142
Malus transitoria	W.Kansu,Tibetan country, SW Choni	1911	322
Malus transitoria	South of Peling mountains		1046
Meconopsis integrifolia	W. Kansu	1911	692
Meconopsis punicea	W. Kansu	1911	698
Meconopsis quintuplinervia	Shensi, Tai-pei-shan	1910	414
Meconopsis quintuplinervia	W. Kansu	1911	709
Melia azedarach	Shensi, Hancheng-hsien	1910	321
Neillia sinensis	Shensi, Tai-pei-shan	1910	1 & 467
Paeonia delavayi	Shensi, Tai-pei-shan	1910	
Paeonia rockii ssp. taibaishanica	Shensi, Tai-pei-shan	1910	1128
Paeonia suffruticosa v.spontanea	Shensi, Yenan-fu	1910	338
Picea meyeri	W. Kansu, Tao river	1911	790
Picea meyeri	Wutai-shan, Shensi	1910	144
Picea meyeri	Kansu, Taochow	1911	790
Picea meyeri	Kansu, Choni	1911	813
Picea wilsonii	Shansi, Wutai-shan	1909	145
Picrasma quassoides	Shensi, Hancheng-hsien	1910	362
Pistacia chinensis	Shensi, Tai-pei-shan	1910	

Platycodon grandiflorum	Chihli, Weichang	1909	112
Platycladus orientalis	N. China		355
Polemonium caeruleum	Shensi, Tai-pei-shan	1910	649
Populus purdomii	Shensi,Tai-pei-shan	1910	1110/1
Populus tomentosa (alba?)	Shensi, Hancheng-hsien	1910	377
Potentilla fruticosa	Chihli, Weichang	1909	127
Potentilla v. veitchii	Shensi, Tai-pei-shan slopes	1910	396/396a
Potentilla v. veitchii	Kansu, Tao River valley	1911	819
Primula geraniifolia	Chihli, Weichang	1909	27
Primula handeliana	Shensi, Tai-pei-shan	1910	397
Primula maximowiczii	Shansi, Wutai-shan	1909	10
Prinsepia uniflora	Shensi, Yenan Fu	1910	324
Prunus davidiana	Shensi, Yenan Fu	1910	347
Prunus padus	Chihli, N.Weichang	1909	238
Prunus tomentosa	Shensi, Tai-pei-shan	1910	3
Quercus dentata	Chihli, East Jehol	1910	273/274
Quercus mongolica	Chili, West Weichang	1910	105/114
Quercus mongolica	Shensi, Hancheng-hsien	1910	333B
Rhamnus davurica	Chihli, Weichang	1910	29
Rhododendron fastigiatum	Shensi, Tai-pei-shan	1910	440
Rhododendron micranthum	Shensi, Tai-pei-shan	1910	2
Rhododendron purdomii	Shensi, Tai-pei-shan	1910	4
Rodgersia aesculifolia	Shensi, Tai-pei-shan	1910	393
Rosa bella	Shansi, Mountains north west	1910	314
Rosa omeiensis	Shensi, Tai-pei-shan	1910	430
Rosa omeiensis	Kansu, Minchow district		1056/1126
Rosa xanthina	Shensi Yenan-fu	1910	339
Salix matsudana	Chihli	1909	65
Schisandra sphenanthera			1037
Smilax discotis	Shensi,Tai-pei-shan	1910	1098

Sorbaria kirilowii	Kansu W.		1018
Sorbus hupehensis	Kansu W., Minchow		1034
Sorbus koehneana	By Tibetan from over border	1910	1121
Sorbus koehneana	Shensi, Tai-pei-shan, western slopes	1910	4/433
Staphylea holocarpa	Shensi, NW of Hancheng Hsien	1910	316/365
Staphylea holocarpa	Shensi,Tai-pei-shan	1910	446
Syringa microphylla	Shensi,Tai-pei-shan	1910	583
Tetracentron sinense	Shensi. Tai-pei-shan	1910	669/670
Thermopsis lanceolata		1909	13
Thuya orientalis	Shensi, Yenan fu	1910	355
Tilia laetivirens	Kansu, Lotani	1911	1070
Tilia mandschurica	Chihli, Weichang	1909	53 & 53a
Tilia mongolica	Chihli, Weichang	1910	86/864
Tilia mongolica	Chihli, Cal-ceen-wong	1910	67
Trollius chinensis	Chihli, Weichang	1909	80
Tsuga chinensis	Shensi, Tai-pei-shan, S slopes	1910	668
Ulmus davidiana	Chihli, South of Weichang	1910	262
Ulmus pumila	Chihli, Weichang	1910	96
Ulmus pumila	Chihli, Cal-ceen-wong	1910	61
Veratrum nigrum			4
Viburnum erubescens var. gracilipes	Shensi, Tai-pei-shan	1910	483/483a
Viburnum fragrans	Kansu, Minchow	1911	689/690
Viburnum kansuense	Shensi, Tai-pei-shan	1910	416
Vitis piasezkii	Shensi, Hancheng-hsien,	1911	372
Zabelia biflora	Shensi, Hancheng-hsien	1910	320a

The Kansu Expedition

The plants from the Kansu Expedition listed below carry Farrer's numbers e.g. F222. Farrer freely admitted that the expedition could not have succeeded without Purdom but wrote to Professor Balfour at the RBGE that he felt his name should be the only one to appear as collector; after all it was *his* expedition. Then he seems to have wavered and taken care to indicate in his field notes (many of which were published by the RHS) which plants were found by Purdom.

NAME	LOCATION	DATE	F. No.
Allium cyaneum	Tibetan border – general & variable	1914	222
Aster farreri	Meadows Bao-u-go/Datung Alps	1914/5	174/582
Buddleja alternifolia	Naindzai to Lodanee	1914	100
Clematis macropetala	Tien Tang Ghyll, Datung Alps	1914?	559
Daphne tangutica	Tibet	1914	271
Dipelta elegans	Chago	1914	18
Dipelta floribunda	Siku	1915	157
Gentiana farreri	Thundercrown	1914	807
Geranium farreri	Min S'an 13-15,000 ft	1914	201
Incarvillea grandiflora	Wolvesden	1915	509
Iris ensata	Loess & road sides	1914	29
Lonicera syringantha	Alps opposite Joni	1914	189
Meconopsis prattii	Min S'an	1914	136
Meconopsis punicea	Valley bottoms opposite Joni	1914	175
Meconopsis quintuplinervia	Satanee/Da Tung Alps	1914/5	118
Meconopsis racemosa	Serchim Alps & Kweite	1915	691
Paeonia woodwardii	Thundercrown	1914	67
Staphylea holocarpa v rosea			57
Stellera chamaejasme	Siku Hills	1914	112
Trollius farreri	Chebson/Hsi-Ling	1915	532
Viburnum fragrans	Wei-yuan-pu	1915	13

It must be remembered that Farrer was primarily interested in alpine plants of quality. When he considered a tree or shrub had particular charm he would collect it, e.g. *Viburnum fragrans* or *Daphne tangutica*. Only a few examples are listed in the table opposite.

The naming of *Meconopsis* species is undergoing major review so the names listed in the Kansu Expedition table (opposite) are those used by Farrer and the modern equivalent may be quite different.

An article about Farrer, his art, language and expeditions to China and Burma was published by the the Alpine Garden Society and subsequently appeared as a bound limited edition of 250 copies in about 1923. The plant photographs from Kansu included in the article were taken by Purdom:

> The Society is indebted to Mr and Mrs Purdom, of Brathay Lodge, Westmorland, for permission to include numerous hitherto unpublished photographs taken by their son during the expedition. Many of the plants were photographed *in situ*, others after removal to the base at Siku.

One of Farrer's major works *The English Rock Garden* (2 vols.) includes even more of Purdom's photographs. Written in 1913 he corrected the proof while they over-wintered in Lanchow in 1914. It was finally published in June 1919. In the introduction Farrer does not hesitate to make his views clear.

In response to criticism by those who considered the over collection of alpines was tantamout to devastating the mountains and exterminating rare plants, Farrer replied:

> More nonsense is talked about collecting alpines, perhaps, than about any other subject in the garden. Even about myself, I am told, are spread a number of legends, always ignorant, and occasionally malicious.

He also resisted vigorously any use of 'common names' for plants; a question still asked today:

> It is perfectly absurd to pretend that there can be a common English name for Alpine species that are neither English nor common.

Purdom photographs of some of the plants collected on the Kansu expedition.

Courtesy Royal Botanic Garden Edinburgh: Farrer Archive, RJF/1/3/1

F112 Stellera chamaejasme   F13 Viburnum fragrans   F175 Meconopsis punicea

F509 Incarvillea grandiflora   F559 Clematis macropetela   F174 Aster farreri

F691 Meconopsis racemosa   F118 Meconopsis quintuplinervia   F807 Gentiana farreri

The Plants

Colour photographs of some plants collected by Purdom and Farrer, mainly in the Lakeland Horticultural Society Garden

Decaisnea fargesii

Aster albescens

Staphylea holocarpa v. rosea

Euonymus alatus with gentians

Dipelta floribunda

Clematis macropetala

Stellera chamaejasme (Yunnan)

Incarvillea sp. (Yunnan)

*Meconopsis quintuplinervia
courtesy Mrs P. Murphy*

Meconopsis punicea   Buddleja alterniflora   Daphne giraldii

Deutzia rubens   Indigofera amblyantha

Hydrangea longipes, courtesy of Mrs. S. Newman.

Malus transitoria (three images above)

Syringa microphylla

Dipteronia sinensis

Potentilla fr. William Purdom

Betula albo sinensis septentrionalis P 752

Rhododendron purdomii   © *Royal Botanic Garden Edinburgh Herbarium E00001283*

The flower colour varies considerably with the season. Sometimes the buds are palest pink, other times far deeper, but normally opening to white.

P1111 Populus purdomii © Royal Botanic Garden Kew Herbarium K000592065

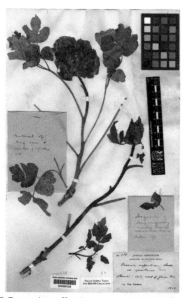

P338 Paeonia suffruticosa v. spontanea © Royal Botanic Garden Kew Herbarium K000687229

Paeonia rockii ssp taibaishanica © President and Fellows of Harvard College. Arnold Arboretum Herbarium.

Aconitum taipeicum © Royal Botanic Garden Kew Herbarium K000076909

Primula handeliana © Royal Botanic Garden Edinburgh Herbarium E00247347

Quercus mongolica © Royal Botanic Garden Edinburgh Herbarium E000242254

Tilia laetivirens © Royal Botanic Garden Edinburgh Herbarium E00008330

Euonymus alatus v pilosus © Royal Botanic Garden Edinburgh Herbarium E00275682

Appendix I
Brothers and Sisters

Information based on the memories of local people, now long passed away, and various historical documents such as census records.

Given their modest beginnings William senior and wife Jane did give their children the best start in life they could. It was no mean achievement to bring up a family of seven children at the end of the nineteenth century. Of the three boys one became a plant collector, a second a Park Superintendent and a third built a new life in Canada. Of the girls, the first became a secondary school headmistress, the second an Inspector of Schools in Malaysia, the third was a nurse and seems to have stayed at the family home all her life but it was she who donated plants and photographs to the Lakeland Horticultural Society (which inspired this book) and the fourth about whom little is known.

MARGARET PURDOM, 1878-1966

Was a teacher for most of her working life. Described in her later years as well-built and stocky, she had a wonderful voice, singing in the Brathay Church choir whenever at home. She had no children.

By 1901 she had become an elementary school teacher boarding in Cambridge Street, London. She taught at St Michael's School, Pimlico for most, if not all, of her professional life. In 1903 the school had over 1,000 pupils of all ages. Margaret was already listed as being a school mistress there in 1905. A local rumour said she taught the future Dame Edith Evans and it could well be true as Dame Edith attended the school until 1903. According to the 1911 census she had moved to new lodgings at 204 Buckingham Palace Road, which she shared with sister Nellie, who was by then an elementary school teacher. It continued to be her home for more than 20 years. She eventually became Head Mistress of a secondary school in London, most probably St Michael's.

She was William's greatest support in the early years, taking care of his finances when he was in China and being on hand during his time at Kew. According to the *Westmorland Gazette* of 19 November 1921 she was in Peking at the time of his death. However this might be a misprint, as Nell was teaching in China at the time.

In April 1929 she set sail on the *Rajputana* for Penang, Malaysia. It can only be assumed to stay with Nell. She did not return to London until four months later. In 1931, aged 53, she married Robert Storey (68) whom she had known for so long. Robert came from Milnthorpe, near Heversham, where Margaret had been born. They lived in Bishops Mansions, Fulham until his death in 1935. Shortly afterwards she moved back to Brathay Lodge to live with Elsie.

During the 1950s she taught at Brathay Church Sunday School and wrote several booklets about the area including:

Associations Clappersgate and Brathay	1958
Associations of Clappersgate and Brathay cont'd	1965

Margaret died at Stanley Hospital, Ulverston on 4 May 1966.

HARRY ALLISON PURDOM, 1882-1975

Followed in his father's footsteps and became a gardener and then park superintendent. He is commemorated on the seat donated to the Lakeland Horticultural Society by sister Elsie 'For Three Native Lakeland Gardeners, William Purdom and sons William and Harry'.

According to the census of 1901 he worked at Rug Hall, a stately home in Corwen, Merionethshire. At that time his future wife Annie J. Wesley, a tailoress, born in 1880, lived in Kettering. In 1908 they married in Amersham and three years later had moved to Church Street, Market Deeping, Lincolnshire where he again worked as a gardener. The others recorded on the census were his wife Annie J. Purdom, dressmaker, and a general domestic servant aged fifteen.

By 1939 they had moved to Worthing, Sussex, where Harry was a head gardener and Annie J. stayed at home for 'domestic duties'. Annie J. died in Kettering in 1956 at the age of 76.

In 1957 Harry Allison Purdom appears on a list of electors in Burton Latimer, near Kettering. By 1969 he had moved to Brixham, Devon. He died in Broomborough Hospital, Totnes, Devon, on 17 December 1975, aged 93 and described as a retired park superintendent.

ANNIE PURDOM, 1884-1971

Annie has left little trace. The local Brathay comment was that she just went away. According to the 1911 Census she worked as an assistant confectioner to Jowetts in Long Preston, near Settle. In 1912 she had a son and then moved to Kettering where she worked again as a confectioner (Kelly's Directory). In 1915 she married Joseph E. Collins and had a daughter in 1916. By 1969 she had moved to an Old People's Home in Kettering. She died in Kettering in 1971. As Harry also lived in Kettering around that time, they surely must have met.

GILBERT HARRISON PURDOM 1886-1958

According to the 1901 Census Gilbert, aged fourteen, was still at home in Brathay Lodge. His school record indicated his attendance at school had been very good.

In 1907 he made his first visit to Canada, leaving Liverpool on the *Victorian* for Halifax, Nova Scotia with the aim of reaching Winnipeg. His trade recorded as carpenter (unclear). The impression given by a local Brathay neighbour was that he seemed to cut himself off from his family. By 1909 he had returned to England and that year married Maud Elizabeth Speight somewhere in or near Rochdale. They appear to have emigrated in 1911 to Winnipeg. By 1921 they had three sons: Lawrence, Reginald and Clarence.

According to one of his daughters-in-law he too had inherited a love of plants and created a beautiful garden. He died in Canada in 1958.

NELLIE PURDOM, 1889-1985

Of all the children Nell (Nellie) had the most extraordinary life. She attended Kelsick School in Ambleside and by 1911 had joined her sister Margaret in London as an elementary school teacher.

From 1917 to 1921 she lived and travelled in North and Central China, Manchuria and Mongolia. She stayed for a year in Peking, from autumn 1917 to autumn 1918 with her beloved brother 'Billiam'. In 1921 she was a teacher in Kuling – a summer and winter resort mainly for American and British missionaries, some of whom became permanent residents.

In August 1922 she returned to Margaret at 204 Buckingham Palace Road, London via Kobe, Japan, on the *Hokozaki Maru*. Barely four months later she was on board the *Glenade* heading for Singapore, as a teacher. From then onwards she crossed and recrossed the Pacific; progressing to First Class accommodation and giving her occupation as School Inspectress and her permanent address as the Federation Malay Straits.

On 31 October 1936 'Miss Nell Purdom, Principal of the Malay Girls' Training Centre married George C. Irving of the Survey Department, 'in the presence of a large and distinguished gathering'. The church (Christ Church) Malacca, was decorated with pink orchids and ferns and the bride wore a dress of silver lamé, with embossed roses and a fishtail train nearly six feet long, lamé shoes, and a wreath of orange blossom. The bride's pupils formed an archway of palm fronds. The reception was held in the Residency. (*The Straits Times*, 1st November 1936).

George was an Australian and in June 1937 they travelled First Class from Sydney to San Francisco, crossed the USA and then sailed to Southampton on the *Queen Mary*. On the way out Nell was described as a College Principal; on the return journey as a housewife. They continued to live and work in Malaya. Nell recalled the fall of Singapore to the Japanese; a desperately dark time for them both. Working on special duties in Singapore, George was taken prisoner-of-war and was interned as a civilian for three and a half years until 1945. (*The Australian Surveyor*, September 1978, Vol 29, No. 3)

Nell described her life as one of constant travel including Bombay, Penang, Brunei (where she served under the Colonial Office of Malay Girls' and Women's education). One tour of duty took her for a month to the Phillipines – before the Americans had left. She wrote cheerfully that money was of no concern as she travelled everywhere in a chauffeur driven car with a lady companion.

In January 1948 she arrived in London from Hong Kong on the *Canton* again First Class with her employment recorded as Education: Malaya. Her destination – as listed – was with sister Elsie, Brathay Lodge. In August she left Southampton with George on the *Oranje* bound for Singapore. In March 1951 she was again on her way alone to London on the *Chusan* leaving from Penang; described as Education Office: Malaya and with Brathay listed as her destination. She returned to Sydney this time by Tourist Class in early July.

By 1954 George and Nell were living in Queensland, Australia, and had moved to Killara, New South Wales, by 1968, then to St Lucia by 1972 where they stayed for the rest of their lives. She visited relatives in Canada with George and one of them described what great care she took of him, even though she was ten years older than he was. 'Tiny... like a little bird... very dainty and a lady' is how she was remembered.

George died in 1978 aged 78 and was buried in Toowong Cemetery, Brisbane. They had been married for almost 42 years. He called her 'Kewpie'. Nell died in 1985 aged 96 and was buried with George. She and George published three books privately – all limited editions: *Run Out Thy Race* (1966); *Sweet Stone Bridge* (1967); *They Change Their Sky* (1969).

SARAH ELSIE PURDOM 1893-1976

Very little is known of Elsie. She lived the greater part of her life her life at Brathay Lodge. Being the youngest she might have stayed at home to look after her parents. She was certainly a Hospital Trained Nurse and one source said she had been a private nurse to a young boy. In the late 1920s she lived in what seems to have been a substantial property in Reigate, Surrey, where the family had four children. Completely different to Nell and Margaret she was described as tall and slim. She kept in touch with her Canadian relatives and in later years helped Nell with family research.

She too inherited a love of plants, particularly alpines, and the garden at Brathay Lodge was once described as a sea of blue gentians. In the 1970s she became one of the earliest members of the Lakeland Horticultural Society and donated a seat and several plants in memory of her father and brothers Harry and William plus the photograph albums of William's travels in China.

As she grew older her sight failed. She was planning to move into a nursing home in Kirkby Lonsdale, but died suddenly of pneumonia in 1976 before she was able to do so. She is buried with her parents and sister Margaret in Brathay Churchyard.

APPENDIX II
People by the Way

Some of the characters included in this book may not be well known. Brief details follow which could not readily be included in the main text.

Sir Alexander Hosie, 1853-1925

Born in Inverurie, Aberdeenshire; his father (a farmer) died when he was only sixteen. He paid his way through university (King's College, Aberdeen) by taking pupils and helped his mother raise his younger brother. He graduated in 1872. After four years as sub-librarian he joined the Chinese consular service. He trained as an interpreter in Peking. He travelled widely in China under dangerous conditions. His first book *Three years in Western China,* (1889) was followed in 1901 by *Manchuria.* From 1908-12 he was consul-general in Tientsin, where he met Purdom in 1909.

Concern over the proliferation of the opium poppy from India into China led to him being employed as commissioner to oversee the eradication of poppy growing in China. *On the Trail of the Opium Poppy* in two volumes was published in 1914. He married Dorothea Soothill in 1913 and retired to the Isle of Wight

Lady Dorothea Hosie, 1885-1959

The second wife of Sir Alexander Hosie, Purdom's sister wrote of her as Miss 'Sutile' – an indication of the pronunciation of her name. Born in China, she was educated in England from 1892 and studied medieval and modern languages at Cambridge.

Her father William Edward Soothill and mother Lucy (Farrar) were both missionaries of the United Methodist Church in China. Her first aim was to study medicine but this changed when she saw how the education of upper class Chinese girls was so neglected. She opened a school in Peking with Miss Bowden-Smith as senior partner.

Soon afterwards the October 1911 revolution disrupted the country. Purdom was able to bring her and her mother to safety in Peking. Dorothea fell in love with Sir Alexander Hosie, 32 years her senior, soon after he retired from the Consular Service in China. She left China in mid-1912 and married Sir Alexander in January 1913. They settled on the Isle of Wight near her husband's brother.

She nursed Sir Alexander until he died in 1925. After the death of both her parents she travelled widely; giving lectures on and writing books about China. Her involvement with the Methodist Church continued until her own death. Amongst her publications were: *Two Gentlemen of China* (1924). When her mother Lucy Soothill died in 1931 Dorothea edited her reminiscences, *Passport to China* (1931) and *Brave New China* (1938)

George Ernest Morrison, 1862-1920

Born in Australia, before he was 21 he had walked from Geelong to Adelaide, a distance of about 600 miles; studied medicine (it seems sporadically) at Melbourne University; canoed down the Murray River, a distance of about 1,650 miles in 65 days; sailed to the South Seas and on return at the end of 1882 decided to walk across Australia from Queensland to Melbourne. He travelled alone, on foot all the way and covered the 2,043 miles in 123 days. After many life threatening adventures he completed his medical studies in Edinburgh and spent two years as surgeon in an Australian hospital.

By 1897 he had settled into the post that would make his name famous as *The Times* first permanent correspondent in Peking.

In recent years there have been conflicting opinions about how well he performed in this position. In his book *Dragon Lady* (1992) Sterling Seagrove describes him as a handsome, courageous but duplicitous character. Apparently, he never learned Chinese and so had to rely on a wide range of English speaking contacts in administrative positions. He was an expert in cultivating them and kept meticulous details of their misdemeanors in his diaries. Seagrove describes how he tried to reconcile conflicting versions of the same event '...lying ingeniously and without remorse in his articles about China.'

There seem to be two facets to his character; the urbane, respected, worldly wise journalist and the other that needed to be handled with a certain degree of caution. His comments about the disparity in ages when Sir Alexander Hosie married Dorothea in 1912 seem strange, as in the same year he married someone who was 27 years his junior. They had three sons.

He became government adviser to Yuan Shih-k'ai on an attractive salary but in doing so lost a certain degree of his influence outside China once he no longer wrote for *The Times*. Over the years he amassed an impressive library which he sold for £35,000 and which became a valued part of the Oriental Library in Tokyo. When his health began to fail he retired to England and endured various misdiagnoses and treatments with typical courage. He died in 1920 and his wife three years later at the tragically young age of 34.

William Christie, 1870-1955

Born in Scotland and moved to America in 1888. He trained at the Missionary Training Institute and from 1892-1924 served under the Christian and Missionary Alliance in China. After arriving in Shanghai, he spent almost two years in Wuhu and Peking studying Chinese and Tibetan languages. His wife had also arrived in China; their son Robert Milton was born in Kuling in 1902 and William Fordyce in Wuhu in 1903. He eventually travelled to Gansu and the district near the Tibetan border, with the intention of setting up a missionary station. They moved to Zhouni (Choni) and settled in a large Tibetan house, which was apparently haunted. Their third son Peter Brainerd was born in 1906.

In 1907 the Christies were allowed home leave and returned to America where their daughter Hazel was born. They returned to Zhouni in 1909 and renewed their friendship with the local Tibetans. The church was organised and services held throughout the years despite growing unrest. Mrs Christie set up a school of about eight grades; taught the girls to knit and boys could be sent to boarding school in Lintao Xian (Ti Tao Jô) if they showed promise. However the situation was becoming more dangerous. The missionary stations were a haven for foreign travellers, where Purdom met Mr Christie in 1910 and again in 1914. In 1914 they escaped the life threatening attack by the White Wolf's bandits and after great hardship arrived in Minchow. It is extraordinary that the whole family survived, given the deaths of 1,000 at Minchow and 7,000 at Tao-chow.

By the early 1920s the Christies were allowed a third home leave to stay on a friend's ranch in Montana. William Christie was unwell and the children aged 15, 14, 11 and 9. He had on previous occasions asked permission to retire and been turned down. The children's education and safety were a cause for concern. When asked to return to China with his wife they accepted this as their duty but left the children behind in Montana. They finally returned to America in 1924 and took up various duties within the Christian alliance. He retired in 1950 and died in 1955, (*William Christie: Apostle to Tibet,* Howard Van Dyck).

Charles Henry Hough, FRCS, 1855-1933

Born in Cambridge. Trained at St Thomas's Hospital and became house-surgeon at Derby Royal Infirmary and remained in Derby for 25 years becoming a leading practitioner in the county. In 1884 he married Alice Maud Redmayne of Brathay Hall at Holy Trinity Church, Brathay. In 1903 they moved to White Craggs a house he had had built near to his wife's home. Here they lived with their three daughters and supported by a domestic staff of nurse, cook and parlour, house and kitchen maids.

They created a glorious hillside garden together. Sadly Alice died after a brief illness in 1909. During his lifetime the garden at White Craggs was always open to the public and proceeds from its gift box and plant sales were given to good causes.

He dedicated his book *A Westmorland Rock Garden* to his daughter Dorothy writing 'but for whose amazing energy and unselfish devotion there would be no rock garden to write about.'

On moving to White Craggs he had resumed medical practice. When the First World War started a friend (Mr Hedley) had offered the nearby historic mansion of Calgarth Park as a hospital, named as a memorial to his wife Ethel Hedley. Mr Hough was asked to organise the hospital. This took all of his time and he was obliged to give up general practise, except as a consultant. The building was completely remodelled and became an orthopaedic hospital for British officers. After the war it was again redesigned to cater for the needs of crippled children throughout the Lakeland counties. It was a surgical centre and extended to include a gymnasium, treatment rooms, 50 patient beds and accommodation for nursing staff. From 1920 until shortly before his death Dr Hough worked in the administration of the hospital. As a devout Christian he also became a lay preacher in later years. He was Purdom's lifelong mentor and friend.

His obituary in the *British Medical Journal* of 21 October 1933, recalls: 'The deep and abiding faith which ordered all his actions was there for everyone to see. In the last few years, as his body became more frail, the spirit of serenity shone... To see him sitting amidst a blaze of colour, high up in his rock garden, gazing across the lake to the distant mountain peaks, was a moving scene...'

Frank N. Meyer, 1875-1918
Born Frans Nicholas Meijer in Amsterdam, he became at the age of fourteen a gardener's assistant at the Amsterdam Botanical Gardens, under Hugo de Vries. After about five years he had risen to head gardener of the experimental garden. De Vries encouraged him to learn French and English as well as the sciences.

He emigrated to the USA in 1901 and became an American citizen in 1908 with the name Frank N. Meyer. In 1901 he started work at the United States Department of Agriculture and then progressed to its plant introduction unit. During the following four years he travelled alone to Mexico, California and Cuba; where necessary working in garden nurseries to pay his way.

Plant collector and future friend David Fairchild asked him to go to East Asia to find plants of economic value for the United States Department of Agriculture. Like Purdom, Meyer went to China alone. He described himself as a pessimist who found it difficult to relax and as a result avoided human contact. This might explain Farrer's impression of him.

His energy was extraordinary. From first expedition (1905-08) he sent back the Chinese persimmon, *Juniperis chinensis* 'Columnaris', *Catalpa bungei*, *Aesculus chinensis* and Ginkgo biloba, plus thousands of vegetable seeds.

His next three expeditions (1909-11, 1912-15 and 1916-18) would be equally productive. He travelled as far west as Russian Turkestan and east into Manchuria, Korea and Kansu (where he met Purdom and Farrer), and collected tens of thousands of specimens; soya beans, grains, fruit, vegetables, bamboos and water chestnuts. He also collected ornamental plants like *Syringa meyeri*, *Juniperus squamata var. meyeri*, *Ulmus parvifolia*, *Ulmus pumila*, *Pyrus calleryana*, *Castanea mollisima*, and *Pistacia chinensis*.

By 1918, with the political situation in China so dangerous, he took a boat down the Yangste to Shanghai, apparently with intention of returning to America. The circumstances of his death have been a subject of speculation. Was it an accident or murder? He was last seen leaving his cabin on 1st June at 11:20 pm. On 5 June his body was found some 50km from the city of Wuhu by a Chinese sailor. He was buried in Shanghai on 12 June. His family in the Netherlands, were notified of his death.

Augustine Henry, 1857-1930

Born in Dundee, he was a brilliant scholar achieving a first class degree at Queen's College, Galway followed by an MA in Belfast and a year studying medicine in London. Aged about 22 he was recruited by Sir Robert Hart to join the Imperial Maritime Customs Service in China. Having completed his medical qualifications and obtained a working knowledge of Chinese, he left for China in 1881. At first he was based in Shanghai and then moved as medical officer to Yichang.

During his spare time he collected Chinese flora sending specimens to Kew. He married while on leave in 1891 and returned to China shortly afterwards. A few years later his wife died of tuberculosis in Colorado, where it had been hoped the climate would be beneficial to her. In 1908 he married for a second time – a happy association which would last until his death in 1930.

Although he is credited with few introductions, he was instrumental in the introduction of *Davidia involucrata*. He had seen it in flower in 1888 and sent herbarium specimens and fruit to Kew. Three men, whom Purdom was later to meet, (Harry Veitch of Veitch Nurseries; Charles Sprague Sargent of the Arnold Arboretum and Ernest Wilson of Kew) planned an expedition to send Wilson to China in 1899 to find the *Davidia*.

Although he had been invited to join this expedition Henry was already feeling the strain of the long time spent in China, saying that the isolation and 'friendlessness' weighed heavily upon him. He was looking forward to his next leave in 1900. However, he would gladly give Wilson all the advice and help he could.

Returning home, he spent time at Kew cataloguing his collections, studying trees at the French National School of Forestry and was joint author with Henry John Elwes of *Trees of Great Britain and Ireland* (in seven volumes). He was also involved in setting up the Chair of Forestry at Cambridge University. Purdom had met him in 1909. They clearly shared the love of and interest in trees, which was to occupy the rest of Purdom's life. Frank Meyer visited him in 1912, before his expedition to China, but their meeting did not seem congenial.

He collected more than 15,000 herbarium specimens and in later years was recognised as a world forestry expert. His own collection of 10,000 tree specimens was given to the National Botanic gardens at Glasnevin, Dublin.

The Brathay Trust

The Brathay Trust, whose headquarters are situated in the house and grounds of Brathay Hall, works with over 7,000 young people every year in their communities and on immersive residential programmes in the Lake District. Brathay follows in the foosteps of its founder, Francis Scott, who bought Brathay Hall in 1939 to protect it from development and to devote it to a worthy cause – developing young people. Much has changed since then but Brathay's key focus is still broadly similar; to improve the life chances of children, young people and families. They do this by inspiring them to engage positively in their communities to make real, life long, change. (Courtesy of the Brathay Trust).

Ingleborough Hall Outdoor Education Centre

The Hall – once the home of Reginald Farrer – is located in eight acres of private grounds in the village of Clapham, in the Yorkshire Dales National Park. The Education Centre specializes in activities for primary and secondary age pupils in adventure education, personal development and environmental studies. Some instructors are nationally qualified in mountain activities or caving and others qualified teachers.

APPENDIX III
Place Names

The maps in this book are intended only as simple guides to Purdom's travels and are mainly based on *Stanfords Atlas* of 1917. The place names are those used by Purdom or Farrer. This was not an easy decision. Many maps of the early 1900s varied wildly in their rendition of Chinese place names and locations. Anyone referring to Herbarium samples or collection lists would not find these names on modern maps.

To complicate matters, Farrer had his own idiosyncratic approach to place names; sometimes translating them into English, German or French or if that were not possible trying to approximate the pronunciation. There are also maps in the back of his books *On the Eaves of the World* and *The Rainbow Bridge*.

It is beyond the scope of this book to provide an in depth list of all the variations possible. Some sources consulted include The Edinburgh Geographical Institute: undated map John Bartholemew & Son; Keith Johnston's General Atlas c1910; National Geographic 1945; Stanfords Atlas 1917; Atlas of the Republic of China Vol III 1961; Times Atlas and GeoCentermap of China.

Purdom/Farrer	Variations	Modern
Provinces		
Honan	Ho-nan	Henan
Kansu		Gansu
Shensi	Shaan-hsi	Shaanxi
Shansi	Shan-hsi	Shanxi
Tibet	Hsi-tsang	Xizang
Geographical features		
Gulf of Chihli	Po Hai	Bo Hai
Koko Nor	Tsing Hai, Ku-ku Nor, Ching Hai	Qinghai Hu
Minshan		Die Shan
Tai pei shan		Taibai Shan
Thundercrown		Leigu Shan
Tsinling shan	Nanshan, Chinling shan	Qinling Shan

Place Names

Towns & Cities

Choni	Jôni, Chone	Zhouni
Chungking		Chongqing
Ichang		Yichang
Jehol	Cheng-the	Chengde
Kalgan		Zhangjiakou
Lanchow	Lanchou	Lanzhou
Pekin(g)	Peiping	Beijing
Sian	Changan, Singan-fu	Xian(Xi'an)
Siku		Zhouqu
Sining		Xining
Taiyuan-fu	T'ai-yüan, Yangqu	Taiyuan
Tientsin		Tianjin
Yenan		Yan'an

Personal names are usually easy to identify with the exception of:

The Dowager Empress (The Old Buddha)	Tzu Hsi, T'zŭ_Hsi	Cixi

Appendix IV
Sources and Bibliography

Photographs and Illustrations
Sources and copyright of the images have been indicated wherever possible. Every effort has been made to trace copyright holders, but in the event of any omission or mistake, please contact the publisher, who will ensure corrections will be made in future re-prints.

Many of the photographs are courtesy of the Lakeland Horticultural Society and come from the albums given to the Society by Purdom's sisters. These albums are on loan to the Archives of the Royal Botanic Garden Edinburgh. Written permission must be acquired from the Lakeland Horticultural Society before any of the photographs in the albums can be reproduced or used. The Royal Botanic Garden Edinburgh can assist with this.

CHAPTER 1 – Cumbria and the Purdom Family
The Armitt Trust, Ambleside
Cumbria Archive Service: WDS 7; WDX 1087; WPR 63/11/2/1/1; BDS 58
Local History Unit, Enfield Leisure Services, London: Edmonton Historical Society, Occasional Paper No 45: 1983
The Lakes Herald, January 1886
Brathay and Ambleside Church Records, The Armitt Trust, Ambleside
The Brathay Trust
Trustees of the Royal Botanic Garden, Kew: 920 DAL *A Gardener's Reminisces* (an unpublished manuscript).
Henry Swainson Cowper: *Hawkshead*, Bemrose & Sons Limited, 1899
Eileen Jay: *The Armitt Story*, Titus Wilson, Kendal, 1998

CHAPTER 2 – Kew 1902-8
The Journal of the Kew Guild: V4s29p63; V5s43p499; V3s21p133; V9s84p748; V2s13p227; V2s15p347; V2s16p399; V2s12p167; V2s11p109
Trustees of the Royal Botanic Garden, Kew: Archive: Staff file of William Purdom; Kew Student Gardeners (1907-1946) f.186-232
Ray Desmond, *The History of the Royal Botanic Gardens KEW*, Harvill Press, 1995

Ray Desmond and F. Nigel Hepper, *A Century of Kew Plantsmen,* Kew Guild, 1993
Richmond and Twickenham Times, 13 February 1909: London Borough of Richmond
  upon Thames: Library and Information Services: Local Studies

CHAPTER 3 – Becoming a Plant Collector
© President and Fellows of Harvard College, Arnold Arboretum Archives: William
  Purdom Papers
Shirley Heriz Smith, *The House of Veitch,* 2002.
Trustees of the Royal Botanic Garden, Kew: as in Chapter 2

CHAPTER 4 – China and the End of Empires
Aisin Goro Pu Yi: *From Emperor to Citizen*, 2 vols, Foreign Language Press, Beijing,
  1986
Sterling Seagrave: *Dragon Lady,* Vintage Books, New York, 1992
Edward Behr: *The Last Emperor,* Macdonald & Co., 1987
Reginald F. Johnson: *Twilight in the Forbidden City,* Oxford University Press, 1985
Jung Chang: *Empress Dowager Cixi*, Jonathon Cape, 2013
The Empress Tzu-hsi: *SC-GR-257 1900, Yu Xunling, Smithsonian Institute*
Yuan Shih-k'ai: *Rio V. De Sieux: The Worlds Work Vol. 30. New York: Doubleday, Page
  & Company, 1915, p. 378*

CHAPTER 5 – The First Expedition 1909-1912
© President and Fellows of Harvard College, Arnold Arboretum Archives: William
  Purdom Papers
The Biodiversity Heritage Library
The Gardeners' Chronicle
Francis H. Nichols: *Through Hidden Shensi,* Charles Scribner & Sons, 1902
Octavia Salkeld: *Daisy's Diary,* Titus Wilson, Kendal, 1993
A. R. Colquhoun: *The 'Overland' to China,* Harper and Brothers, London, 1900
Henri Borel: *The New China,* T. Fisher Unwin, 1912
'Filices Purdomianae' in *The Botanical Gazette,* Vol. 56, No. 4, pps 331-8.

CHAPTER 6 – Difficult Years
David Fairchild: *The World Was My Garden,* Charles Scribner & Sons, 1938
Isabel Shipley Cunningham: *Frank N. Meyer,* The Iowa State University Press, 1990
The Royal Geographic Society
© President and Fellows of Harvard College, Arnold Arboretum Archives: William
  Purdom Papers
The Gardeners' Chronicle, 4 October 1913, 'Plant collecting in China by Mr. Purdom',
  The Biodiversity Heritage Library.

CHAPTER – 7 Farrer's Plan
Mrs Joan Farrer
Charles Henry Hough: *A Westmorland Rock Garden*, Frederick Middleton, Ambleside, 1948
Royal Botanic Garden Edinburgh Library: Farrer Archive

CHAPTER 8 – The Kansu Expedition 1914-15
Royal Botanic Garden Edinburgh: Farrer Archive
Mrs Joan Farrer
Biodiversity Heritage Library
The Wellcome Trust
The Gardeners' Chronicle
Reginald Farrer: O*n the Eaves of the World* (2 vols), Edward Arnold & Co., 1926 and *The Rainbow Bridge*, Edward Arnold & Co., 1921

CHAPTER 9 – Staying On
Royal Botanic Garden Edinburgh: Farrer Archive
Mrs Joan Farrer
Royal Horticultural Society, Lindley Library: PUR William Purdom: papers relating to work in China 1909-c.1921
The John Rylands University Library: *The North China Herald,* 12 November 1921
State Library, New South Wales: G. E. Morrison: MLMSS 312

CHAPTER 10 – Forgotten and Remembered
Cumbria Archive Service Kendal: WDX 1087
Jigongshan National Park, Henan, China
Purdom Forest Park, Henan, China

CHAPTER 11 – The Plant Collections
Biodiversity Heritage Library
The Gardeners' Chronicle
Royal Botanic Gardens Kew Herbarium
Royal Botanic Gardens Kew Library and Archives
Royal Botanic Garden Edinburgh Herbarium
Smithsonian Institute Herbarium
© President and Fellows of Harvard College, Arnold Arboretum*: Arnoldia*
The Royal Horticultural Society Journal 1914 and 1915
The Royal Horticultural Society, *2017 Plantfinder*
The Royal Horticultural Society, Lindley Library
Selected Bibliography
Aisin Goro Pu Yi: *From Emperor to Citizen*, 2 vols, Foreign Language Press, Beijing
Mea Allan: *E.A.Bowles & his garden at Myddelton House,* Faber & Faber, 1975

Sources and Bibliography

W. J. Bean: *Trees and Shrubs Hardy in the British Isles*, John Murray, 1951
Edward Behr: *The Last Emperor,* Macdonald & Co., 19871986
Henri Borel: *The New China,* T. Fisher Unwin, 1912
Ursula Buchan: *An Anthology of Garden Writing,* Croom Helm, 1986
Tom Fletcher Bunin: *Life in Langdale*, Titus Wilson, Kendal, 1993
Jung Chang: *Empress Dowager Cixi*, Jonathon Cape, 2013
Alice M Coats: *The Quest for Plants,* Studio Vista, 1969
P. D. Coates: *The China Consuls,* Oxford University Press, 1988
A. R. Colquhoun: *The 'Overland' to China,* Harper and Brothers, London, 1900
Henry Swainson Cowper: *Hawkshead*, Bemrose & Sons Limited, 1899
E. M. H. Cox: *Plant Hunting in China,* The Scientific Book Guild, 1945
E. M. H. Cox: *The Plant Introductions of Reginald Farrer,* New Flora and Silva Ltd., 1930
Barbara Crossley: *The Other Ambleside*, Titus Wilson, Kendal, 2000
Isabel Shipley Cunningham: *Frank N. Meyer*, The Iowa State University Press, 1984
Daniel Defoe: *A Tour thro' the Whole Island of Great Britain*, 1724-27
Ray Desmond & F. Nigel Hepper: *A Century of Kew Plantsmen*, The Kew Guild, 1993
Ray Desmond: *A History of the Royal Botanic Gardens KEW*, The Harvill Press, 1995
Charles & Bessie Ewing: *Death Throes of a Dynasty*, The Kent State University Press, 1990
Howard Van Dyck: *Apostle to Tibet,* Christian Publications Inc, Harrisburg Pa., 1956
David Fairchild: *The World Was My Garden,* Charles Scribner's Sons, 1938
Reginald Farrer: *On the Eaves of the World*, Edward Arnold & Co., 1926
Reginald Farrer: *Rainbow Bridge*, Edward Arnold & Co., 1921
Reginald Farrer: *The Void of War,* Houghton Mifflin Company, 1918
F. H. Fisher: *Reginald Farrer*, The Alpine Garden Society, limited edition Vol.1 No. 10.
Margaret Fitzherbert: *The Man Who was Greenmantle,* Oxford University Press
Hilliers: *The Hillier Manual of Trees and Shrubs,* 1991 edn
Alexander Hosie: *On the Trail of the Opium Poppy*, G. Philip & Son, 1914
Charles Henry Hough: *A Westmorland Rock Garden*, Frederick Middleton, Ambleside 1948
John Illingworth & Jane Routh: *Reginald Farrer*, Centre for North-West Regional Studies, University of Lancaster, 1991
Brian Inglis: *The Opium War,* Hodder and Stoughton Limited, 1976
Eileen Jay: *The Armitt Story*, Titus Wilson, Kendal, 1998
Reginald F. Johnson: *Twilight in the Forbidden City,* Oxford University Press, 1985
Lo Hui-Min (Ed): *The Correspondence of G. E. Morrison,* Cambridge University Press, 1976
Brenda McLean: *A Pioneering Plantsman*, The Stationery Office, 1997
Brenda McLean: *George Forrest*, Antique Collectors' Club, 2004
W. R. Mitchell: *Reginald Farrer,* Castleberg, 2002

Christopher Morris (Ed): *The Illustrated Journeys of Celia Fiennes 1685-1712*, Macdonald & Co.. 1982

Francis H Nichols: *Through Hidden Shensi*, Charles Scribner & Sons, 1902

William Woodville Rockhill: *The Land of the Lamas*, Longmans, 1891

Royal Horitcultural Society: *Plant Finder,* 2017

Octavia Salkeld: *Daisy's Diary*, Titus Wilson Kendal, 1993

Charles Sprague Sargent Ed: *Plantae Wilsonianae,* 3 Vols Cambridge University Press, 1913-1917

Sterling Seagrave: *Dragon Lady,* Vintage Books, New York, 1992

Philip W. Sergeant: *The Great Empress Dowager of China,* Hutchinson, 1910

Sue Shepherd: *Seeds of Fortune*, Bloomsbury Publishing Plc, 2003

Nicola Shulman: *A Rage for Rock Gardening*, Short Books, 2001

Osbert Sitwell: *Noble Essences,* Macmillan & Co Ltd, 1950

F. C. Stern: *A Chalk Garden*, Faber & Faber, 1974

Sir Eric Teichman: *Travels of a Consular Officer,* Cambridge University Press, 1921

H. F. Wallace: *The Big Game of Central & Western China,* Antony Rowe Ltd, 1913

Marina Warner: *The Dragon Empress,* Sphere Books Ltd, London, 1974

Acknowledgements

The Lakeland Horticultural Society, Holehird Gardens, Windermere, Cumbria above all deserves my greatest thanks – without it my interest in William Purdom would never have arisen; in particular the 'Friday Gardeners' and all 'Holehirders' who suffered my endless ramblings about William Purdom over the years with such infinite patience.

Others who deserve a special mention are: the Arnold Arboretum especially Head of Library and Archives Lisa Pearson; Joe Melanson (who copied and airmailed items in times before information existed on the web) and Beth Bailey; the Royal Botanic Gardens Edinburgh, in particular, Graham Hardy for his kind help and support over so many years; Leonie Paterson Archivist and Head Librarian and the Herbarium; the Royal Botanic Gardens Kew Archives and Library and especially Craig Brough; the Kew Herbarium, Dr Sarah Phillips and team; Sparkle Ward Editor of *The Journal of the Kew Guild*; the Royal Geographic Society; the Library of New South Wales; the Smithsonian Institute; the Royal Horticultural Society Lindley Library; John Scott of J S Graphics; Cumbria Archive Services; Kendal Local History Library; Deborah Walsh Curator, Armitt Museum and Archive, Ambleside; the British Library Photographic section; Gary Dunlop ; Chris Sanders; Dr and Mrs Joan Farrer; Alan Purdom; Reg Purdom; Nicola Shulman; Caradoc Doy (Veitch expert); Heather Jones of the Brathay Trust; Tim Hutchinson; Michael Rank; Francois Gordon (researching Purdom with particular interest in the political/diplomatic issues of the time); and friends whose encouragement and shared knowledge is deeply appreciated. Not forgetting, Dawn Robertson of Hayloft Publishing who kept me going when my confidence failed.

A special thanks to my friend Mei Yonghong (Purdom researcher) and all met in Xinyang in 2008. In particular the custodians of Purdom Forest Park and Jigongshan Nature Reserve and the Tourist Authority of Xinyang who have ensured that the name of William Purdom will not be forgotten in the China he loved so much.

Index